100
POEMS

100
POEMS

ॐ ॐ ॐ ॐ ॐ ॐ

SELECTED AND EDITED
WITH AN INTRODUCTION
AND GLOSSARY BY

A. J. M. Smith

Granger Index Reprint Series

BOOKS FOR LIBRARIES PRESS SS
PLAINVIEW, NEW YORK

INTERNATIONAL STANDARD BOOK NUMBER:

0-8369-6203-6

LIBRARY OF CONGRESS CATALOG CARD NUMBER:

73-133073

PRINTED IN THE UNITED STATES OF AMERICA

ACKNOWLEDGMENTS

The following pages constitute an extension of the copyright page.

J. M. DENT & SONS LTD. "A Winter's Tale" reprinted from *Deaths and Entrances* by Dylan Thomas by permission of J. M. Dent & Sons and the Literary Executors of the Dylan Thomas Estate.

FABER & FABER LTD. "The Hollow Men" and "Gerontion" from *Collected Poems, 1901-1962* by T. S. Eliot.

"September 1, 1939" from *Collected Shorter Poems by W. H. Auden* by W. H. Auden.

HARCOURT, BRACE & WORLD "The Hollow Men" and "Gerontion" from *Collected Poems, 1909-1962* by T. S. Eliot, copyright 1936, by Harcourt, Brace & World, Inc.; 1963, 1964 by T. S. Eliot. Reprinted by permission of the publishers.

HARVARD UNIVERSITY PRESS "Because I Could Not Stop for Death" by Emily Dickinson from *The Poems of Emily Dickinson* edited by Thomas H. Johnson, by permission of the publishers.

To the Reader

This is a book of samples. It is a short and representative selection of the best poems written in English from the end of the Middle Ages to the present. It would be absurd of course to claim that this is THE hundred best poems in the language or indeed to think that such a collection could possibly be made. These are all good poems, however, and most of them (in spite of the wide differences in style, mood, tone, attitude, and genre) are by any standard great poems.

This is a book of poems, and it is better to talk at first about poems rather than about poetry, though I should think it would hardly be possible to read right through these hundred poems without acquiring some knowledge of poetry in general and, if good will is there, a heightened feeling for it.

Let me set down a few axioms. Some readers may like to consider them now; others may prefer to wait until they have read a good many of the poems. The readers this book is mainly intended for are students in their first year of college, most of whom are not specialists in 'English' and whose acquaintance with great poems of earlier times has been limited or casual. For such it may be better to pick up knowledge and acquire a skill in reading by going directly to the poems. Then when interest has been stimulated and curiosity aroused the student may like to check his impressions with some of the assertions and judgments set down here at the beginning.

First, it should be recognized that no matter what the ultimate purpose of a poem may be that purpose can only be achieved insofar as it gives pleasure. "If the prospect of delight be wanting," as John Dryden said, the poem will never be read and its purpose not even suspected. In a collection of *good* poems, however, there is the prospect of many kinds of pleasure—from emotional involvement to the intellectual excitement that may come from seeing a difficult or intricate problem in emotional dynamics neatly solved. Keats' "Ode to a Nightingale" gives us the one sort of pleasure, Marvell's "To his Coy Mistress" the other; and there are almost as many sorts of pleasure in between as there are poems.

Now for some axioms, dogmatic articles, which have helped the compiler select the particular great poems that make up this book.

Making poems is a human and personal activity.

Poetry is both expression and communication.

Poetry is a form of speech, and while its raw material is experience, the medium is language. It is an ordering of words. Ezra Pound has defined poetry as *news that stays news*.

A poet, as the word is derived from the Greek and as Chaucer named him, is a maker. A poem is something made, and like a chair or a table, it is shaped by conscious craftsmanship. It doesn't just come as an unexpected and undeserved free gift of the Muses.

Now we may consider the poem as expression and concentrate on the maker—his experience, his intention, the quality of his sensibility, and his technical proficiency. Or we may consider the poem as a thing in itself, an artifact having an independent and objective existence—not an 'imitation of nature' at all but a new and unique thing that must justify its own being as a new and beautiful impingement upon our perceptions. This is the view Archibald MacLeish is taking when he tells us that "A poem should not mean/But be" and that William Carlos Williams illustrates when he makes a complete poem out of the single statement:

> so much depends
> upon
>
> a red wheel
> barrow
>
> glazed with rain
> water
>
> beside the white
> chickens

or presents a ball game as a poem—a poem that everyone feels and understands:

> The crowd at the ball game
> is moved uniformly
>
> by a spirit of uselessness
> which delights them—

all the exciting detail
of the chase

and the escape, the error
the flash of genius—

all to no end save beauty
the eternal.

This is the concept of the poem as a self-justifying thing-in-itself, a living and delightful object. The printed or written poem, it must be said, is only the script. The poem itself is the vibrations of the sounds on the air and in the eardrum as it is read aloud and heard, or the indentations of the mind as it is absorbed—ultimately, that is, a psychological stimulus, a mental and emotional ballet.

Or again, we may consider the poem as communication.

Like other works of art, as distinguished from contributions to knowledge, editorials, timetables, digests of science, and expository prose generally, a poem is indivisibly and at the same time both what is communicated and the instrument of communication. It is at once the telegraph wire, the electric current, and the message transmitted. But it is not the man who sends it, and not, of course, the man (if any) who receives it.

It is to this problematical and ideal recipient, the proverbial "dear reader," you yourself whoever you are, that we must turn for a moment.

There is indeed an ideal reader or listener as well as an ideal poet and an ideal poem; and it is useful to think about them all and to consider the qualities and virtues of each. The reader has responsibilities just as the poet has. Let us think for a moment what they are.

The first rule of what might be called "good readership"—at least with respect to poetry—is to approach the poem with an open (but not an empty) mind. A poem has been defined, accurately enough, if a little pedantically, as a highly organized, complex, and unified re-creation of an experience; and it aims to communicate to the receptive reader a new experience, analogous to the one out of which the poet made his poem. Furthermore, a poem makes use of the widest variety of the rich and subtle resources of language, while at the same time it utilizes also a number of special techniques having to do with rhythm, harmony, and figurative language. It is not reasonable to expect that what depends on subtlety, complexity, nuance and suggestion should be immediately, easily, and completely available to every casual uninstructed cursory inspection. The reader, indeed, should be prepared to give to the assimilation of a mature poem something of the same diligent and loving care that a student of music gives to a fugue of Bach or a sonata of Beethoven.

One of the first difficulties that the uninstructed or the misinstructed reader finds before him lies in the distinctiveness of much poetic language. Poetic language is a form of picture-writing; it is essentially figurative, making frequent use of metaphor and simile, image and symbol to *suggest* what cannot be stated and to convey the emotional correlative of a thought rather than the naked thought itself. Poetic language differs from the language of science or fact in that it implies or suggests more or less than it states, and sometimes indeed achieves an effect of irony or significant ambiguity by a suggestion or a tone that is in sharp contrast to the literal assertion. It uses sound effects and picturesque images, fantastic comparisons and metaphysical conceits, striving "to apprehend," as Theseus in *A Midsummer Night's Dream* put it, "More than cool reason ever comprehends."

Many people (even many who habitually use slang, which when original and new is one of the purest forms of poetic language) often fail to interpret figurative language imaginatively or, what is commoner, as the experiment described in I. A. Richards' *Practical Criticism* demonstrates, translate it too literally. There is the story (probably apocryphal) of the student in Freshman English who interpreted Keats' line "Heard melodies are sweet, but those unheard are sweeter" as "It's nice to listen to music, but it's nicer not to." That is an extreme case, but many ordinary readers find themselves in the same sort of difficulty when they read in Shelley that

> Life like a dome of many-coloured glass
> Stains the white radiance of eternity

or in T. S. Eliot that

> the evening is spread out against the sky
> Like a patient etherised upon a table.

If there is a failure of communication here I am not suggesting that any moral obloquy attaches to the common reader or any conviction of sin is to be brought home to him. Far from it. I am only saying that the prejudice against the complexity and the imaginative or impressionistic richness of much mature poetry is very widespread (and quite understandable) but that if the causes of that prejudice are understood it can be cleared up—at least for readers who are willing to learn to read with their senses alert and their imagination awake. This is not an easy task, but it is an important one.

The widespread ignorance of the language of poetry and of art in general has some serious consequences. What they are in their most general terms was stated by the English critic F. R. Leavis. The arts, he began by assuming, are something more than a luxury product—they are the "storehouse of recorded values" and, in consequence, "there is a necessary relationship between the quality of the individual's response to art and his general fitness for humane existence." The most disastrous result from the point of view of the incompetent reader is a general impoverishment of life, an inability to partake of the rich banquet that the poets and artists, *those whose ideas are always at the tip of their senses,* spread before him.

The sensuous and imaginative richness of language, a richness that enhances and is enhanced by real depth of thought, gives poetry its essential quality. Poetry is language purified of the superficial, and whether we find it in Chaucer, Donne, Pope, or Dylan Thomas we can detect its hard, sharp, concentrated intensity—an intensity of thought and feeling that cannot be separated. "Literature" (poetry, that is), said Ezra Pound, "is language *charged* with meaning"—charged as a battery is charged with electricity, bristling with energy, and loaded with significance. And this is true of even the gentlest poem.

Here in our hundred poems we have all moods and tones, tender and bitter, savage and gentle, serene and passionate, angry and resigned, but what they all have in common is a devotion to the truth of the poet's feeling and a technical mastery adequate to the task of communicating that truth accurately and powerfully.

But a great poem demands a great reader. It is to help the student become such a reader that these poems are offered for his consideration and, the editor hopes, for his delight.

CONTENTS

xiv

100
POEMS

1 ◆ *Western Wind, When Wilt Thou Blow*

Western wind, when wilt thou blow,
The small rain down can rain?
Christ, if my love were in my arms,
And I in my bed again!

2 ◆ *The Falcon*

Lully, lulley! lully, lulley!
The faucon hath borne my make away!

He bare him up, he bare him down,
He bare him into an orchard brown.

In that orchard there was an halle,   5
That was hangèd with purple and pall.

And in that hall there was a bed,
It was hangéd with gold so red.

And in that bed there li'th a knight,
His woundès bleeding day and night.   10

At that bed's foot there li'th a hound,
Licking the blood as it runs down.

By that bed-side kneeleth a may,
And she weepeth both night and day.

And at that bed's head standeth a stone,   15
Corpus Christi written thereon.

2. *make*: mate.   13. *may*: maid.

3

Lully, lulley! lully, lulley!
The faucon hath borne my make away.

3 ⸱ The Twa Corbies

As I was walking all alane,
I heard twa corbies making a mane;
The tane unto the t' other say,
"Where sall we gang and dine today?"

5 "In behint yon auld fail dyke,
I wot there lies a new-slain knight;
And naebody kens that he lies there,
But his hawk, his hound, and lady fair.

"His hound is to the hunting gane,
10 His hawk to fetch the wild-fowl hame,
His lady's ta'en another mate,
So we may mak our dinner sweet.

"Ye'll sit on his white hause-bane,
And I'll pick out his bonny blue een;
15 Wi' ae lock o' his gowden hair
We'll theek our nest when it grows bare.

"Mony a one for him makes mane,
But nane sall ken where he is gane;
O'er his white banes when they are bare,
20 The wind sall blaw for evermair."

4 ⸱ Sir Patrick Spens

The king sits in Dumferling toune,
   Drinking the blude-reid wine:
O quhar will I get guid sailor,
   To sail this schip of mine?

2. *corbies:* ravens.   *mane:* moan.   5. *fail:* earthen.   6. *wot:* know.
7. *kens:* knows.   13. *hause-bane:* neck bone.   16. *theek:* line.
18. *sall:* shall.   3. *quhar:* where.

Up and spak an eldern knicht,   5
    Sat at the king's richt knee:
Sir Patrick Spens is the best sailor
    That sails upon the sea.

The king has written a braid letter,
    And signed it wi' his hand;   10
And sent it to Sir Patrick Spens,
    Was walking on the sand.

The first line that Sir Patrick red,
    A loud lauch lauchéd he:
The next line that Sir Patrick red,   15
    The teir blinded his ee.

O quhar is this has don this deid,
    This ill deid don to me;
To send me out this time o' the yeir,
    To sail upon the sea?   20

Mak haste, mak haste, my mirry men all,
    Our good schip sails the morn.
O say na sae, my master deir,
    For I feir a deadlie storme.

Late late yestreen I saw the new moone   25
    Wi' the auld moone in hir arme;
And I feir, I feir, my deir master,
    That we will come to harme.

O our Scots nobles wer richt laith
    To weet their cork-heild schoone;   30
But lang owre a' the play were played,
    Their hats they swam aboone.

O lang, lang may the ladies stand
    Wi' their fans into their hand,
Or e'er they see Sir Patrick Spens   35
    Come sailing to the land.

14. *lauch*: laugh.   29. *laith*: loth.   32. *aboone*: about.

5

O lang, lang, may the ladies stand
    Wi' their gold kems in their hair,
Waiting for their ain deir lords,
40   For they'll see them na mair.

Have owre, have owre to Aberdour,
    It's fifty fadom deip:
And thair lies guid Sir Patrick Spens,
    Wi' the Scots lords at his feit.

5 ✦ *Edward, Edward*

I

"Why does your brand sae drop wi' blude,
    Edward, Edward?
Why does your brand sae drop wi' blude,
    And why sae sad gang ye, O?"—
5   "O I hae kill'd my hawk sae gude,
    Mither, mither;
O I hae kill'd my hawk sae gude,
    And I had nae mair but he, O."

II

"Your hawk's blude was never sae red,
10   Edward, Edward;
Your hawk's blude was never sae red,
    My dear son, I tell thee, O."—
"O I hae kill'd my red-roan steed,
    Mither, mither;
15   O I hae kill'd my red-roan steed,
    That erst was sae fair and free, O."

III

"Your steed was auld, and ye hae got mair,
    Edward, Edward;
Your steed was auld, and ye hae got mair;
20   Some other dule ye dree, O."

41. *have owre:* half way over.   1. *brand:* sword.
20. *dule:* sorrow.   *dree:* mourn or suffer.

"O I hae kill'd my father dear,
   Mither, mither;
O I hae kill'd my father dear,
   Alas, and wae is me, O!"

IV

"And whatten penance will ye dree for that,   25
   Edward, Edward?
Whatten penance will ye dree for that?
   My dear son, now tell me, O."—
"I'll set my feet in yonder boat,
   Mither, mither;   30
I'll set my feet in yonder boat,
   And I'll fare over the sea, O."

V

"And what will ye do wi' your tow'rs and your ha',
   Edward, Edward?
And what will ye do wi' your tow'rs and your ha',   35
   That were sae fair to see, O?"—
"I'll let them stand till they doun fa',
   Mither, mither;
I'll let them stand till they doun fa',
   For here never mair maun I be, O."   40

VI

"And what will ye leave to your bairns and your wife,
   Edward, Edward?
And what will ye leave to your bairns and your wife,
   When ye gang owre the sea, O?"—
"The warld's room: let them beg through life,   45
   Mither, mither;
The warld's room: let them beg through life;
   For them never mair will I see, O."

VII

"And what will ye leave to your ain mither dear,
   Edward, Edward?   50

27. *dree:* suffer or pay.   49. *ain:* own.

7

And what will ye leave to your ain mither dear,
   My dear son, now tell me, O?"—
"The curse of hell frae me sall ye bear,
   Mither, mither;
The curse of hell frae me sall ye bear:
   Sic counsels ye gave to me, O!"

6 ┊ Clerk Saunders

Clerk Saunders and may Margaret
   Walk'd owre yon garden green;
And deep and heavy was the love
   That fell thir twa between.

"A bed, a bed," Clerk Saunders said,
   "A bed for you and me!"
"Fye na, fye na," said may Margaret,
   "Till anes we married be!"

"Then I'll take the sword frae my scabbárd
   And slowly lift the pin;
And you may swear, and save your aith,
   Ye ne'er let Clerk Saunders in.

"Take you a napkin in your hand,
   And tie up baith your bonnie e'en,
And you may swear, and save your aith,
   Ye saw me na since late yestreen."

It was about the midnight hour,
   When they asleep were laid,
When in and came her seven brothers,
   Wi' torches burning red;

When in and came her seven brothers,
   Wi' torches burning bright:
They said, "We hae but one sister,
   And behold her lying with a knight!"

53. *frae*: from.

Then out and spake the first o' them, 25
  "I bear the sword shall gar him dee."
And out and spake the second o' them,
  "His father has nae mair but he."

And out and spake the third o' them,
  "I wot that they are lovers dear." 30
And out and spake the fourth o' them,
  "They hae been in love this mony a year."

Then out and spake the fifth o' them,
  "It were great sin true love to twain."
And out and spake the sixth o' them, 35
  "It were shame to slay a sleeping man."

Then up and gat the seventh o' them,
  And never a word spake he;
But he has striped his bright brand
  Out through Clerk Saunders' fair body. 40

Clerk Saunders he started, and Margaret she turn'd
  Into his arms as asleep she lay;
And sad and silent was the night
  That was atween thir twae.

And they lay still and sleepit sound 45
  Until the day began to daw';
And kindly she to him did say,
  "It is time, true love, you were awa'."

But he lay still, and sleepit sound,
  Albeit the sun began to sheen; 50
She look'd atween her and the wa',
  And dull and drowsie were his e'en.

Then in and came her father dear;
  Said, "Let a' your mourning be;
I'll carry the dead corse to the clay, 55
  And I'll come back and comfort thee."

"Comfort weel your seven sons,
    For comforted I will never be:
I ween 'twas neither knave nor loon
    Was in the bower last night wi' me."

60

The clinking bell gaed through the town,
    To carry the dead corse to the clay;
And Clerk Saunders stood at may Margaret's
        window,
    I wot, an hour before the day.

65

"Are ye sleeping, Margaret?" he says,
    "Or are ye waking presently?
Give me my faith and troth again,
    I wot, true love, I gied to thee."

"Your faith and troth ye sall never get,
70   Nor our true love sall never twin,
Until ye come within my bower,
    And kiss me cheik and chin."

"My mouth it is full cold, Marg'ret;
    It has the smell, now, of the ground;
75 And if I kiss thy comely mouth,
    Thy days of life will not be lang.

"O cocks are crowing a merry midnight;
    I wot the wild fowls are boding day;
Give me my faith and troth again,
80   And let me fare me on my way."

"Thy faith and troth thou sallna get,
    And our true love sall never twin,
Until ye tell what comes o' women,
    I wot, who die in strong traivelling?"

85 "Their beds are made in the heavens high,
    Down at the foot of our good Lord's knee,
Weel set about wi' gillyflowers;
    I wot, sweet company for to see.

"O cocks are crowing a merry midnight;
　I wot the wild fowls are boding day;　　　　　　90
The psalms of heaven will soon be sung,
　And I, ere now, will be miss'd away."

Then she has taken a crystal wand,
　And she has stroken her troth thereon;
She has given it him out at the shot-window,　　95
　Wi' mony a sad sigh and heavy groan.

"I thank ye, Marg'ret; I thank ye, Marg'ret;
　And ay I thank ye heartily;
Gin ever the dead come for the quick,
　Be sure, Marg'ret, I'll come for thee."　　　　100

It's hosen and shoon, and gown alone,
　She climb'd the wall, and follow'd him,
Until she came to the green forest,
　And there she lost the sight o' him.

"Is there ony room at your head, Saunders?　　105
　Is there ony room at your feet?
Or ony room at your side, Saunders,
　Where fain, fain, I wad sleep?"

"There's nae room at my head, Marg'ret,
　There's nae room at my feet;　　　　　　　　110
My bed it is fu' lowly now,
　Amang the hungry worms I sleep.

"Cauld mould is my covering now,
　But and my winding-sheet;
The dew it falls nae sooner down　　　　　　　115
　Than my resting-place is weet.

"But plait a wand o' bonny birk,
　And lay it on my breast;
And shed a tear upon my grave,
　And wish my saul gude rest."　　　　　　　　120

11

Then up and crew the red, red cock,
    And up and crew the gray;
" 'Tis time, 'tis time, my dear Marg'ret,
    That you were going away.

125 "And fair Marg'ret, and rare Marg'ret,
    And Marg'ret o' veritie,
Gin e'er ye love another man,
    Ne'er love him as ye did me."

GEOFFREY CHAUCER   1340?-1400

7 ꝭ FROM THE *Prologue* TO *The Canterbury Tales*

Whan that Aprille with his shoures soote
The droghte of March hath perced to the roote,
And bathed every veyne in swich licour
Of which vertu engendred is the flour;
5   Whan Zephirus eek with his sweete breeth
Inspired hath in every holt and heeth
The tendre croppes, and the yonge sonne
Hath in the Ram his half cours yronne,
And smale foweles maken melodye,
10   That slepen al the nyght with open eye
(So priketh hem nature in hir corages):
Than longen folk to goon on pilgrymages,
And palmeres for to seken straunge strondes,
To ferne halwes, kouthe in sondry londes;
15   And specially from every shires ende
Of Engelond to Caunterbury they wende,
The holy blisful martir for to seke,
That hem hath holpen whan that they were seeke.

1. *soote*: sweet.   3. *swich*: such.   5. *Zephirus*: the west wind.
8. *Ram*: Aries, a sign of the Zodiac.   9. *foweles*: birds.
11. *priketh*: inspires.   *corages*: hearts.
13. *palmeres*: pilgrims.   *straunge strondes*: foreign shores.
14. *ferne halwes*: distant shrines.   *kouthe*: well-known.
17. *martir*: St. Thomas à Becket.   18. *seeke*: sick.

Line numbers: throughout this selection the line numbers are given as in the complete poem.

Bifel that, in that sesoun on a day,
In Southwerk at the Tabard as I lay   20
Redy to wenden on my pilgrymage
To Caunterbury with ful devout corage,
At nyght was come into that hostelrye
Wel nyne and twenty in a compaignye,
Of sondry folk, by aventure yfalle   25
In felaweshipe, and pilgrymes were they alle,
That toward Caunterbury wolden ryde.
The chambres and the stables weren wyde,
And wel we weren esed atte beste.
And shortly, whan the sonne was to reste,   30
So hadde I spoken with hem everichon,
That I was of hir felaweshipe anon,
And made forward erly for to ryse,
To take oure wey ther as I yow devyse.

* * * * * * * *

A Knyght ther was, and that a worthy man,
That fro the tyme that he first bigan
To riden out, he loved chivalrye,   45
Trouthe and honour, fredom and curteisye.
Ful worthy was he in his lordes werre,
And ther-to hadde he riden, no man ferre,
As wel in Cristendom as in hethenesse,
And evere honoured for his worthynesse.   50
At Alisaundre he was whan it was wonne.
Ful ofte tyme he hadde the bord bigonne
Aboven alle nacions in Pruce.
In Lettow hadde he reysed and in Ruce,
No Cristen man so ofte of his degree.   55
In Gernade at the seege eek hadde he be
Of Algezir, and riden in Belmarye.
At Lyeys was he and at Satalye,
Whan they were wonne; and in the Grete See

25. *aventure:* chance.   28. *wyde:* spacious.   29. *esed:* entertained.
34. *devyse:* tell.   46. *fredom:* generosity.   47. *lordes werre:* king's war.
48. *ferre:* farther.   51. *Alesaundre:* Alexandria.
52. *the bord bigonne:* presided at the head of the table.   53. *Pruce:* Prussia.
54. *reysed:* campaigned.   *Ruce:* Russia.   59. *Grete Sea:* the Mediterranean.

At many a noble armee hadde he be.
At mortal batailles hadde he been fiftene,
And foghten for oure feith at Tramyssene
In lystes thries, and ay slayn his foo.
This ilke worthy knyght hadde been also
Som-tyme with the lord of Palatye,   65
Agayn another hethen in Turkye.

    And evere-moore he hadde a sovereyn prys;
And though that he were worthy, he was wys,
And of his port as meke as is a mayde.
He nevere yet no vileynye ne sayde   70
In al his lyf un-to no maner wight.
He was a verray, parfit gentil knyght.

    But for to tellen yow of his array,
Hise hors were goode, but he was nat gay.
Of fustian he wered a gypoun   75
Al bismotered with his habergeoun,
For he was late ycome from his viage,
And wente for to doon his pilgrymage.

    With hym ther was his sone, a yong Squyer,
A lovere and a lusty bachelor,   80
With lokkes crulle, as they were leyd in presse.
Of twenty yeer of age he was, I gesse.

    Of his stature he was of evene lengthe,
And wonderly delyvere, and of greet strengthe.
And he hadde been som-tyme in chivachye   85
In Flaundres, in Artoys, and Picardye,
And born hym wel, as of so litel space,
In hope to stonden in his lady grace.

    Embrouded was he, as it were a meede
Al ful of fresshe floures, white and reede.   90
Syngynge he was, or floytynge, al the day;
He was as fressh as is the monthe of May.
Short was his gowne, with sleves longe and wyde.

---

63. *lystes:* lists.   64. *ilke:* same.   67. *prys:* reputation.   72. *verray:* true.
75. *fustian:* coarse cloth.   *gypoun:* vest.
76. *bismotered:* stained.   *habergeoun:* coat of mail.   81. *crulle:* curled.
84. *delyvere:* agile.   85. *chivachye:* cavalry raids.
89. *Embrouded:* embroidered.   91. *floytynge:* playing the flute.

Wel koude he sitte on hors and faire ryde.
He koude songes make and wel endite,   95
Juste and eek daunce, and wel purtreye and write.
So hoote he lovede, that by nyghtertale
He slepte namoore than dooth a nyghtyngale.
   Curteys he was, lowely, and servysable,
And carf biforn his fader at the table.   100
   A Yeman hadde he and servantz namo
At that tyme, for hym liste ryde so;
And he was clad in coote and hood of grene.
A sheef of pecok arwes bright and kene
Under his belt he bar ful thriftily,   105
(Wel koude he dresse his takel yemanly:
His arwes drouped noght with fetheres lowe),
And in his hand he bar a myghty bowe.
A not heed hadde he, with a broun visage.
Of wodecraft wel koude he al the usage.   110
Upon his arm he bar a gay bracer,
And by his syde a swerd and a bokeler,
And on that oother syde a gay daggere,
Harneysed wel and sharp as poynt of spere,
A Cristofre on his brest of silver shene.   115
An horn he bar, the bawdryk was of grene;
A forster was he, soothly, as I gesse.
   Ther was also a nonne, a Prioresse,
That of hir smylyng was ful symple and coy;
Hir gretteste ooth was but by Seint Loy;   120
And she was cleped Madame Eglentyne.
   Ful wel she soong the servyce dyvyne,
Entuned in hir nose ful semely,
And Frenssh she spak ful faire and fetisly,
After the scole of Stratford-atte-Bowe,   125

---

96. *juste:* joust.　　97. *by nyghtertale:* at night.　　101. *namo:* no more.
102. *hymn liste ryde so:* he chooses to ride so.　　104. *Arwes:* arrows.
109. *not heed:* a head brown and grizzled like a nut.
114. *Harneysed:* mounted.
115. *A Cristofre:* an image of the patron saint of archers.
116. *bawdryk:* belt.　　117. *forster:* forester, game-keeper.
120. *Seint Loy:* St. Louis.　　121. *cleped:* called.　　124. *fetisly:* elegantly.

For Frenssh of Parys was to hire unknowe.
  At mete wel ytaught was she with alle:
She let no morsel from hir lippes falle,
Ne wette hir fyngres in hir sauce depe.
130   Wel koude she carie a morsel and wel kepe
That no drope ne fille up-on hir brest.
In curteisie was set ful muchel hir lest.
Hir over lippe wyped she so clene
That in hir coppe ther was no ferthyng sene
135   Of grece, whan she dronken hadde hir draughte.
Ful semely after hir mete she raughte.
And sikerly she was of greet desport,
And ful plesaunt, and amyable of port,
And peyned hire to countrefete cheere
140   Of court, and to been estatlich of manere,
And to been holden digne of reverence.
  But, for to speken of hir conscience,
She was so charitable and so pitous
She wolde wepe, if that she sawe a mous
145   Caught in a trappe, if it were deed or bledde.
Of smale houndes hadde she, that she fedde
With rosted flessh, or mylk and wastel breed.
But soore wepte she if oon of hem were deed,
Or if men smoot it with a yerde smerte;
150   And al was conscience and tendre herte.
  Ful semely hir wympel pynched was;
Hir nose tretys, hir eyen greye as glas,
Hir mouth ful smal, and ther-to softe and reed;
But sikerly she hadde a fair forheed:
155   It was almoost a spanne brood, I trowe;
For, hardily, she was nat undergrowe.
Ful fetys was hir cloke, as I was war.
Of smal coral aboute hir arm she bar
A peyre of bedes, gauded al with grene,

---

132. *In curteisie . . . hir list:* she set great store by good manners.
134. *ferthyng:* particle.   136. *raughte:* reached.   137. *sikerly:* certainly.
139. *peyned . . . court:* she took pains to imitate courtly manners.
140. *estatlich:* stately.   147. *wastel breed:* fine white bread.
149. *yerde:* stick.   *smerte:* smartly.   151. *pynched:* pleated.
152. *tretys:* shapely.   156. *hardily:* certainly.

And there-on heng a brooch of gold ful shene, 160
On which ther was first writen a crowned A,
And after *Amor vincit omnia.*

* * * * * * * *

A Frere ther was, a wantowne and a merye,
A lymytour, a ful solempne man.
In alle the ordres foure is noon that kan 210
So muche of daliaunce and fair langage.
He hadde maad ful many a mariage
Of yonge wommen at his owene cost.
    Un-to his ordre he was a noble post.
Ful wel biloved and famulier was he 215
With frankeleyns over al in his contree,
And with worthy wommen of the toun;
For he hadde power of confessioun,
As seyde hym-self, moore than a curat,
For of his ordre he was licenciat. 220
Ful swetely herde he confessioun,
And pleasaunt was his absolucioun;
He was an esy man to yeve penaunce,
Ther-as he wiste to have a good pitaunce.
For un-to a poure ordre for to yive 225
Is signe that a man is wel yshryve;
For if he yaf, he dorste make avaunt,
He wiste that a man was repentaunt;
For many a man so hard is of his herte,
He may nat wepe, al-thogh hym soore smerte. 230
Ther-fore in stede of wepynge and preyeres,
Men moote yeve silver to the poure freres.
    His typet was ay farsed ful of knyves
And pynnes, for to yeven faire wyves.
And certeynly he hadde a murye note; 235
Wel koude he synge and pleyen on a rote;

162. *Amor . . . omnia:* Love conquers all.
209. *lymytour:* a friar licensed to beg in a limited territory.   210. *kan:* knew.
216. *frankeleyns:* rich country squires.
224. *Ther-as:* where.   *wiste:* knew.   *pitaunce:* gift.
227. *yaf:* gave.   *avaunt:* boast.   233. *typet:* cape.   *ay farsed:* always stuffed.
236. *rote:* a stringed instrument.

Of yeddynges he bar outrely the prys.
His nekke whit was as the flour de lys;
Ther-to he strong was as a champioun.
240   He knew the tavernes wel in every toun,
And every hostiler and tappestere
Bet than a lazar or a beggestere;
For un-to swich a worthy man as he
Accorded nat, as by his facultee,
245   To have with sike lazars aqueyntaunce.
It is nat honeste, it may nat avaunce
For to deelen with no swich poraille,
But al with riche and selleres of vitaille.
And over-al, ther as profit sholde arise,
250   Curteys he was and lowely of servyse.
Ther was no man no wher so vertuous.
He was the beste beggere in his hous,
For thogh a wydwe hadde noght a sho,
So plesant was his *In principio,*
255   Yet wolde he have a ferthyng, er he wente.
His purchas was wel bettre than his rente.
And rage he koude, as it were right a whelpe.
In lovedayes ther koude he muchel helpe:
For ther he was nat lyk a cloystrer
260   With a threadbare cope, as is a poure scoler,
But he was lyk a maister or a pope.
Of double worstede was his semycope,
That rounded as a belle out of the presse.
Somewhat he lipsed, for his wantownesse,
To make his Englissh sweete up-on his tonge;
And in his harpyng, whan that he hadde songe,
Hise eyen twynkled in his heed aright,
As doon the sterres in the frosty nyght.
This worthy lymytour was cleped Huberd.

* * * * * * * *

237. *yeddynges:* ballads.   *outrely:* entirely.   241. *tappestere:* barmaid.
242. *lazar:* leper.   *beggestere:* beggar woman.   246. *honeste:* respectable.
247. *poraille:* poor trash.   248. *vitaille:* victuals.
254. *In principio:* In the beginning, first words of St. John's gospel.
256. *purchas:* graft.   *rente:* regular income.
258. *lovedayes:* days set aside for the settlement of disputes by law.
262. *semycope:* short cape.   264. *lipsed:* lisped.

18

A Clerk ther was oi Oxenford also,   285
That un-to logyk hadde longe ygo.
   As leene was his hors as is a rake,
And he was nat right fat, I undertake,
But looked holwe, and ther-to sobrely.
Ful thredbare was his overeste courtepy;   290
For he hadde geten hym yet no benefice,
Ne was so worldly for to have office.
For hym was levere have at his beddes heed
Twenty bookes, clad in blak or reed,
Of Aristotle and his philosophie,   295
Than robes riche, or fithele, or gay sautrie.
   But al be that he was a philosophre,
Yet hadde he but litel gold in cofre;
But al that he myghte of his frendes hente,
On bookes and on lernynge he it spente,   300
And bisily gan for the soules preye
Of hem that yaf hym wher-with to scoleye.
   Of studie took he moost cure and moost heede.
Noght oo word spak he moore than was neede,
And that was seid in forme and reverence,   305
And short and quyk and ful of heigh sentence.
Sownynge in moral vertu was his speche,
And gladly wolde he lerne and gladly teche.

             *   *   *   *   *   *   *   *

   A good Wyf was ther of biside Bathe,   445
But she was som del deef, and that was scathe.
   Of clooth makyng she hadde swich an haunt,
She passed hem of Ypres and of Gaunt.
In al the parisshe wyf ne was ther noon
That to the offrynge bifore hire sholde goon;   450
And if ther dide, certeyn so wrooth was she,
That she was out of alle charitee.
Hir coverchiefs ful fyne were of ground;
I dorste swere they weyeden ten pound

286. *ygo:* begun.   290. *courtepy:* short coat.
296. *fithele, or gay sautrie:* fiddling or merry music.
299. *hente:* get.   302. *scoleye:* study.   307. *Sownynge:* sounding.
445. *biside:* just outside.   446. *scathe:* a pity.   447. *haunt:* knack.

19

455 That on a Sonday weren up-on hir heed.
 Hir hosen weren of fyn scarlet reed,
 Ful streite yteyd, and shoes ful moyste and newe.
 Boold was hir face, and fair, and reed of hewe.
  She was a worthy womman al hir lyve;
460 Housbondes at chirche dore she hadde fyve,
 With-outen oother compaignye in youthe,—
 But ther-of nedeth nat to speke as nouthe.
  And thries hadde she been at Jerusalem;
 She hadde passed many a straunge strem;
465 At Rome she hadde been, and at Boloyne,
 In Galice at Seint Jame, and at Coloyne.
 She koude muche of wandrynge by the weye.
 Gat tothed was she, soothly for to seye.
  Upon an amblere esily she sat,
470 Ywympled wel, and on hir heed an hat
 As brood as is a bokeler or a targe;
 A foot mantel aboute hir hipes large,
 And on hir feet a peyre of spores sharpe.
 In felawshipe wel koude she laughe and carpe.
475 Of remedies of love she knew par chaunce,
 For she koude of that art the olde daunce.
  A good man was ther of religioun,
 And was a poure Persoun of a toun,
 But riche he was of holy thoght and werk.
480 He was also a lerned man, a clerk,
 That Cristes gospel trewely wolde preche;
 His parisshens devoutly wolde he teche.
 Benygne he was, and wonder diligent,
 And in adversitee ful pacient,
485 And swich he was preved ofte sithes.
  Ful looth were hym to cursen for his tithes,
 But rather wolde he yeven, out of doute,
 Un-to his poure parisshens aboute
 Of his offrynge and eek of his substaunce.

---

462. *as nouthe:* at present.   474. *carpe:* talk.
476. *the olde daunce:* she knew all the tricks of the game.
485. *preved:* proved.   *ofte sithes:* many times.   486. *cursen:* excommunicate.
487. *yeven:* give.

He koude in litel thyng have suffisaunce. 490
Wyd was his parisshe, and houses fer asonder,
But he ne lafte nat, for reyn ne thonder,
In siknesse nor in meschief, to visite
The ferreste in his parisshe, muche and lite,
Up-on his feet, and in his hond a staf. 495
This noble ensampie to his sheep he yaf,
That first he wroghte, and afterward he taughte.
Out of the gospel he tho wordes caughte,
And this figure he added eek ther-to,
That if gold ruste, what sholde iren do? 500
For if a preest be foule, on whom we truste,
No wonder is a lewed man to ruste;
And shame it is, if a preest take keep,
A shiten shepherde and a clene sheep.
Wel oghte a preest ensample for to yive, 505
By his clennesse, how that his sheep sholde lyve.
  He sette nat his benefice to hyre,
And leet his sheep encombred in the myre,
And ran to Londoun, un-to Seint Poules,
To seken hym a chauntrye for soules, 510
Or with a bretherhede to been withholde;
But dwelte at hoom, and kepte wel his folde,
So that the wolf ne made it nat myscarye;
He was a shepherde and noght a mercenarye.
  And thogh he hooly were and vertuous, 515
He was noght to synful men despitous,
Ne of his speche daungerous ne digne,
But in his techyng discreet and benigne.
To drawen folk to hevene by fairnesse,
By good ensample, this was his bisynesse, 520
But it were any persone obstinat,
What so he were, of heigh or lowe estat,
Hym wolde he snybben sharply for the nonys.

494. *muche and lite:* high and low.   502. *lewed:* ignorant.   508. *leet:* left.
510. *a chauntrye for soules:* an endowment for singing requiem masses.
511. *bretherhede:* a guild.   *withholde:* hired as chaplain.
517. *daungerous ne digne:* standoffish nor disdainful.
523. *snybben:* snub or rebuke.   *for the nonys:* right away.

A bettre preest I trowe that nowher noon ys.
525   He wayted after no pompe and reverence,
       Ne maked hym a spiced conscience,
       But Cristes loore, and his apostles twelve,
       He taughte, but first he folwed it hym-selve.

SIR THOMAS WYATT *1503-1542*

8 ⌁ *They Flee from Me*

       They flee from me, that sometime did me seek,
       With naked foot stalking in my chamber.
       I have seen them gentle, tame, and meek,
       That now are wild, and do not remember
5   That sometime they put themselves in danger
       To take bread at my hand; and now they range
       Busily seeking with a continual change.

       Thankéd be fortune it hath been otherwise
       Twenty times better; but once, in special,
10   In thin array, after a pleasant guise,
       When her loose gown from her shoulders did fall,
       And she me caught in her arms long and small,
       Therewithal sweetly did me kiss,
       And softly said, Dear heart, how like you this?

15   It was no dream; I lay broad waking:
       But all is turnéd thorough my gentleness
       Into a strange fashion of forsaking;
       And I have leave to go of her goodness,
       And she also to use newfangleness.
20   But since that I so kindly am servéd,
       How like you this, what hath she now deservéd?

9 ✸ *Prothalamion*

Calm was the day, and through the trembling air
Sweet breathing Zephyrus did softly play,
A gentle spirit, that lightly did delay
Hot Titan's beams, which then did glister fair;
When I, whom sullen care,   5
Through discontent of my long fruitless stay
In princes' court, and expectation vain
Of idle hopes, which still to fly away,
Like empty shadows, did afflict my brain,
Walked forth to ease my pain   10
Along the shore of silver streaming Thames,
Whose rutty bank, the which his river hems,
Was painted all with variable flowers,
And all the meads adorned with dainty gems
Fit to deck maidens' bowers,   15
And crown their paramours
Against the bridal day, which is not long—
    Sweet Thames! run softly, till I end my song.

There, in a meadow, by the river's side,
A flock of nymphs I chancéd to espy,   20
All lovely daughters of the flood thereby,
With goodly greenish locks, all loose untied,
As each had been a bride.
And each one had a little wicker basket,
Made of fine twigs, entrailéd curiously,   25
In which they gathered flowers to fill their flasket,
And with fine fingers cropt full feateously
The tender stalks on high.

Prothalamion: a ceremonial song before a marriage. This poem was written to celebrate the double wedding of two daughters of the Earl of Worcester in the fall of 1596.

2. *Zephyrus:* the south wind.   4. *Titan:* the sun.
20. *nymphs:* young girls. Here portrayed as votaries of the river-god.
25. *entailéd:* intertwined.   27. *feateously:* nimbly, featly.

Of every sort, which in that meadow grew,
30 They gathered some: the violet, pallid blue,
The little daisy, that at evening closes,
The virgin lily, and the primrose true,
With store of vermeil roses,
To deck their bridegrooms' posies
35 Against the bridal day, which was not long—
     Sweet Thames! run softly, till I end my song.

With that I saw two swans of goodly hue
Come softly swimming down along the Lee;
Two fairer birds I yet did never see.
40 The snow, which doth the top of Pindus strew,
Did never whiter shew,
Nor Jove himself, when he a swan would be
For love of Leda, whiter did appear;
Yet Leda was, they say, as white as he,
45 Yet not so white as these, nor nothing near;
So purely white they were,
That even the gentle stream, the which them bare,
Seemed foul to them, and bade his billows spare
To wet their silken feathers, lest they might
50 Soil their fair plumes with water not so fair,
And mar their beauties bright,
That shone as heaven's light,
Against their bridal day, which was not long—
     Sweet Thames! run softly, till I end my song.

55 Eftsoons the nymphs, which now had flowers their fill,
Ran all in haste to see that silver brood,
As they came floating on the crystal flood;
Whom when they saw, they stood amazéd still,
Their wondering eyes to fill;
60 Them seemed they never saw a sight so fair
Of fowls so lovely, that they sure did deem
Them heavenly born, or to be that same pair

40. *Pindus:* a mountain range in northern Greece.
43. *Leda:* became the mother of Helen of Troy by Zeus, or Jove, who made
love to her in the guise of a swan. See Yeats' sonnet "Leda and the Swan."
55. *Eftsoons:* soon afterward.

Which through the sky draw Venus' silver team;
For sure they did not seem
To be begot of any earthly seed, 65
But rather angels, or of angels' breed;
Yet were they bred of summer's heat, they say,
In sweetest season, when each flower and weed
The earth did fresh array;
So fresh they seemed as day, 70
Even as their bridal day, which was not long—
    Sweet Thames! run softly, till I end my song.

Then forth they all out of their baskets drew
Great store of flowers, the honor of the field,
That to the sense did fragrant odors yield, 75
All which upon those goodly birds they threw
And all the waves did strew,
That like old Peneus' waters they did seem,
When down along by pleasant Tempe's shore,
Scattered with flowers, through Thessaly they stream, 80
That they appear, through lilies' plenteous store,
Like a bride's chamber floor.
Two of those nymphs meanwhile, two garlands bound
Of freshest flowers which in that mead they found,
The which presenting all in trim array, 85
Their snowy foreheads there withal they crowned,
Whilst one did sing this lay,
Prepared against that day,
Against their bridal day, which was not long— 90
    Sweet Thames! run softly, till I end my song.

"Ye gentle birds! the world's fair ornament,
And heaven's glory, whom this happy hour
Doth lead unto your lovers' blissful bower,
Joy may you have, and gentle heart's content
Of your love's couplement; 95
And let fair Venus, that is queen of love,
With her heart-quelling son upon you smile,

78. *Peneus:* a river in Thessaly.
79. *Tempe:* a valley in Thessaly sacred to the Muses.
97. *heart-quelling son:* Cupid.

Whose smile, they say, hath virtue to remove
All love's dislike, and friendship's faulty guile
100 Forever to assoil;
Let endless peace your steadfast hearts accord,
And blessed plenty wait upon your board;
And let your bed with pleasures chaste abound,
That fruitful issue may to you afford,
105 Which may your foes confound,
And make your joys redound
Upon your bridal day, which is not long—"
    Sweet Thames! run softly, till I end my song.

So ended she; and all the rest around
110 To her redoubled that her undersong,
Which said their bridal day should not be long.
And gentle Echo from the neighbor ground
Their accents did resound.
So forth those joyous birds did pass along,
115 Adown the Lee, that to them murmured low,
As he would speak, but that he lacked a tongue,
Yet did by signs his glad affection show,
Making his stream run slow.
And all the fowl which in his flood did dwell
120 'Gan flock about these twain, that did excel
The rest, so far as Cynthia doth shend
The lesser stars. So they, enrangéd well,
Did on those two attend,
And their best service lend
125 Against their wedding day, which was not long—
    Sweet Thames! run softly, till I end my song.

At length they all to merry London came,
To merry London, my most kindly nurse,
That to me gave this life's first native source,
130 Though from another place I take my name,
An house of ancient fame.
There when they came, whereas those bricky towers
The which on Thames' broad, aged back do ride,

98. *virtue:* power.   100. *assoil:* absolve.
121. *Cynthia:* the moon.   *shend:* outshine, excel.

26

Where now the studious lawyers have their bowers,
There whilom wont the Templar Knights to bide   135
Till they decayed through pride.
Next whereunto there stands a stately place,
Where oft I gainéd gifts and goodly grace
Of that great lord, which therein wont to dwell,
Whose want too well now feels my friendless case;   140
But ah! here fits not well
Old woes, but joys, to tell
Against the bridal day, which is not long—
    Sweet Thames! run softly, till I end my song.

Yet therein now doth lodge a noble peer,   145
Great England's glory and the world's wide wonder,
Whose dreadful name late through all Spain did thunder,
And Hercules' two pillars standing near
Did make to quake and fear:
Fair branch of honor, flower of chivalry!   150
That fillest England with thy triumph's fame,
Joy have thou of thy noble victory,
And endless happiness of thine own name,
That promiseth the same;
That through thy prowess and victorious arms,   155
Thy country may be freed from foreign harms;
And great Elisa's glorious name may ring
Through all the world, filled with thy wide alarms,
Which some brave muse may sing
To ages following,   160
Upon the bridal day, which is not long—
    Sweet Thames! run softly, till I end my song.

From those high towers this noble lord issuing,
Like radiant Hesper, when his golden hair
In th' ocean billows he hath bathéd fair,   165
Descended to the river's open viewing,

135. There once the Knights Templars used to dwell.
139. *that great lord:* the Earl of Leicester.   145. *noble peer:* the Earl of Essex.
148. *Hercules' two pillars:* Gibraltar and Abyla at the western entrance of the Mediterranean.
157. *great Elisa:* Queen Elizabeth I.   164. *Hesper:* the Evening Star.

With a great train ensuing.
Above the rest were goodly to be seen
Two gentle knights of lovely face and feature
170 Beseeming well the bower of any queen,
With gifts of wit, and ornaments of nature,
Fit for so goodly stature,
That like the twins of Jove they seemed in sight,
Which deck the baldrick of the heavens bright;
175 They two, forth pacing to the river's side,
Received those two fair brides, their love's delight;
Which, at th' appointed tide,
Each one did make his bride
Against their bridal day, which is not long—
180   Sweet Thames! run softly, till I end my song.

10 ⁊ *And Is There Care in Heaven?*
FROM *The Faerie Queene* (II, viii, 1-2)

And is there care in heaven? and is there love
In heavenly spirits to these creatures base,
That may compassion of their evils move?
There is: else much more wretched were the case
5 Of men, than beasts. But O th' exceeding grace
Of highest God, that loves his creatures so,
And all his workes with mercy doth embrace,
That blessed Angels, he sends to and fro,
To serve to wicked man, to serve his wicked foe.

10 How oft do they, their silver bowers leave,
To come to succour us, that succour want?
How oft do they with golden pineons, cleave
The flitting skyes, like flying Poursuivant,
Against foule feends to aid us militant?
15 They for us fight, they watch and dewly ward,
And their bright Squadrons round about us plant,
And all for love, and nothing for reward:
O why should heavenly God to men have such regard?

169. *Two gentle knights:* the two bridegrooms.

11 *1 The Lie*

Go, soul, the body's guest,
  Upon a thankless arrant:
Fear not to touch the best;
    The truth shall be thy warrant.
      Go, since I needs must die,   5
      And give the world the lie.

Say to the court, it glows
  And shines like rotten wood;
Say to the church, it shows
    What's good, and doth no good: 10
      If church and court reply,
      Then give them both the lie.

Tell potentates, they live
  Acting by others' action,
Not loved unless they give,   15
    Not strong but by a faction:
      If potentates reply,
      Give potentates the lie.

Tell men of high condition
  That manage the estate,   20
Their purpose is ambition,
    Their practice only hate:
      And if they once reply,
      Then give them all the lie.

Tell them that brave it most,   25
  They beg for more by spending,
Who, in their greatest cost,
    Seek nothing but commending:
      And if they make reply,
      Then give them all the lie.   30

2. *arrant:* errand.

Tell zeal it wants devotion;
Tell love it is but lust;
Tell time it is but motion;
Tell flesh it is but dust:
35   And wish them not reply,
    For thou must give the lie.

Tell age it daily wasteth;
Tell honour how it alters;
Tell beauty how she blasteth;
40 Tell favour how it falters:
    And as they shall reply,
    Give every one the lie.

Tell wit how much it wrangles
In tickle points of niceness;
45 Tell wisdom she entangles
Herself in over-wiseness:
    And when they do reply,
    Straight give them both the lie.

Tell physic of her boldness;
50 Tell skill it is prevention;
Tell charity of coldness;
Tell law it is contention:
    And as they do reply,
    So give them still the lie.

55 Tell fortune of her blindness;
Tell nature of decay;
Tell friendship of unkindness;
Tell justice of delay:
    And if they will reply,
60   Then give them all the lie.

39. *blasteth:* withers.
44. *tickle:* pernickety, picayune.   *niceness:* over fastidiousness.
49. *Tell physic* etc.: accuse medicine of presumptuousness, pride and irreligion.
61-62. In the arts, reputation not true worth is the source of honors.

30

Tell arts they have no soundness,
 But vary by esteeming;
Tell schools they want profoundness,
 And stand too much on seeming:
  If arts and schools reply,   65
  Give arts and schools the lie.

Tell faith it's fled the city;
 Tell how the country erreth;
Tell, manhood shakes off pity;
 Tell, virtue least preferreth: 70
  And if they do reply
  Spare not to give the lie.

So when thou hast, as I
 Commanded thee, done blabbing,
Although to give the lie   75
 Deserves no less than stabbing,
  Stab at thee he that will,
  No stab the soul can kill.

12 ⸗ *Even Such Is Time*

Even such is Time, that takes in trust
 Our youth, our joys, our all we have,
And pays us but with age and dust;
 Who, in the dark and silent grave,
When we have wandered all our ways,   5
Shuts up the story of our days.
But from this earth, this grave, this dust,
My God shall raise me up, I trust.

70. Proclaim the truth that virtue or merit gets the least preferment. (For a
similar disillusioned point of view see Shakespeare: *Sonnet 66 Tir'd with all
these*.)

Even Such Is Time: Said to have been written in the Tower on the eve of his
execution.

13 ⸗ *Leave Me, O Love*

> Leave me, O Love, which reachest but to dust;
> And thou, my mind, aspire to higher things;
> Grow rich in that which never taketh rust;
> Whatever fades but fading pleasure brings.
> 5   Draw in thy beams, and humble all thy might
> To that sweet yoke where lasting freedoms be;
> Which breaks the clouds and opens forth the light,
> That doth both shine and give us sight to see.
> O, take fast hold! let that light be thy guide
> 10   In this small course which birth draws out to death—
> And think how evil becometh him to slide,
> Who seeketh heaven, and comes of heavenly breath.
>   Then farewell, world; thy uttermost I see:
>   Eternal Love, maintain thy life in me.

CHRISTOPHER MARLOWE *1564-1593*

14 ⸗ *The Passionate Shepherd to His Love*

> Come live with me and be my love,
> And we will all the pleasures prove
> That hills and valleys, dales and fields,
> And all the craggy mountains yields.

> 5   There we will sit upon the rocks
> And see the shepherds feed their flocks,
> By shallow rivers to whose falls
> Melodious birds sing madrigals.

> And I will make thee beds of roses
> 10   With a thousand fragrant posies,
> A cap of flowers, and a kirtle
> Embroidered all with leaves of myrtle;

A gown made of the finest wool
Which from our pretty lambs we pull;
Fair lined slippers for the cold,   15
With buckles of the purest gold;

A belt of straw and ivy buds,
With coral clasps and amber studs;
And if these pleasures may thee move,
Come live with me and be my love   20

The shepherd swains shall dance and sing
For thy delight each May-morning:
If these delights thy mind may move,
Then live with me and be my love

WILLIAM SHAKESPEARE *1564-1616*

Sonnets

15   CXVI

Let me not to the marriage of true minds
Admit impediments. Love is not love
Which alters when it alteration finds,
Or bends with the remover to remove:
O, no! it is an ever-fixéd mark,   5
That looks on tempests and is never shaken;
It is the star to every wand'ring bark,
Whose worth's unknown, although his heighth be taken.
Love's not Time's fool, though rosy lips and cheeks
Within his bending sickle's compass come;   10
Love alters not with his brief hours and weeks,
But bears it out even to the edge of doom:—
     If this be error and upon me proved,
     I never writ, nor no man ever loved.

2. *Admit impediments:* admit that there can be any barrier to the union of
souls, a Platonic idea.
8. *heighth:* height, the altitude giving the position but not the size or quality of
the star.

Th' expense of spirit in a waste of shame
Is lust in action; and till action, lust
Is perjur'd, murd'rous, bloody, full of blame,
Savage, extreme, rude, cruel, not to trust:
5   Enjoy'd no sooner but despiséd straight;
Past reason hunted, and no sooner had,
Past reason hated, as a swallow'd bait
On purpose laid to make the taker mad:
Mad in pursuit and in possession so;
10   Had, having, and in quest to have, extreme;
A bliss in proof, and prov'd, a very woe;
Before, a joy propos'd; behind, a dream.
    All this the world well knows; yet none knows well
    To shun the heaven that leads men to this hell.

Poor soul, the center of my sinful earth,
Thrall to these rebel powers that thee array,
Why dost thou pine within and suffer dearth,
Painting thy outward walls so costly gay?
5   Why so large cost, having so short a lease,
Dost thou upon thy fading mansion spend?
Shall worms, inheritors of this excess,
Eat up thy charge? Is this thy body's end?
Then, soul, live thou upon thy servant's loss,
10   And let that pine to aggravate thy store;
Buy terms divine in selling hours of dross;
Within be fed, without be rich no more:
    So shalt thou feed on Death, that feeds on men,
    And Death once dead, there's no more dying then.

1. *expense:* expenditure.
11. *in proof:* while being experienced.   *prov'd:* after having been experienced.
CXLVI, 2. *rebel powers:* the senses.   *array:* arraign, make guilty, condemn.
    4. *outward walls:* the body.
    6. *fading mansion:* the body, the habitation of the soul subject to age, decay,
    and death.   7. *excess:* wasteful expenditure.
10. *aggravate:* make greater, magnify.

FROM *Love's Labour's Lost*

When icicles hang by the wall,
　And Dick the shepherd blows his nail,
And Tom bears logs into the hall,
　And milk comes frozen home in pail,
When blood is nipp'd, and ways be foul,　　　　5
Then nightly sings the staring owl,
　　　　　To-whit!
To-who!—a merry note,
While greasy Joan doth keel the pot.

When all aloud the wind doth blow,　　　　10
　And coughing drowns the parson's saw,
And birds sit brooding in the snow,
　And Marian's nose looks red and raw,
When roasted crabs hiss in the bowl,
Then nightly sings the staring owl,　　　　15
　　　　　To-whit!
To-who!—a merry note,
While greasy Joan doth keel the pot.

19 ↑ *Song*

FROM *Twelfth Night*

O Mistress mine, where are you roaming?
O stay and hear! your true-love's coming
　That can sing both high and low;
Trip no further, pretty sweeting:
Journeys end in lovers meeting　　　　5
　Every wise man's son doth know.

What is love? 'tis not hereafter;
Present mirth hath present laughter;
　What's to come is still unsure:
In delay there lies no plenty:　　　　10

Then come kiss me, Sweet-and-twenty,
   Youth's a stuff will not endure.

20 ◊ *Song*

   FROM *The Tempest*

         Full fathom five thy father lies;
            Of his bones are coral made;
         Those are pearls that were his eyes:
            Nothing of him that doth fade
5   But doth suffer a sea-change
         Into something rich and strange.
         Sea-nymphs hourly ring his knell:
                              Ding-dong.
         Hark! now I hear them,—Ding-dong, bell.

         THOMAS CAMPION *1567-1620*

21 ◊ *When to Her Lute Corinna Sings*

         When to her lute Corinna sings,
         Her voice revives the leaden strings,
         And doth in highest notes appear,
         As any challenged Echo clear;
5   But when she doth of mourning speak,
         E'en with her sighs the strings do break.

         And as her lute doth live or die,
         Led by her passion, so must I!
         For when of pleasure she doth sing,
10   My thoughts enjoy a sudden spring;
         But if she doth of sorrow speak,
         E'en from my heart the strings do break.

22 / *Song*

Go and catch a falling star,
   Get with child a mandrake root,
Tell me where all past years are,
   Or who cleft the devil's foot,
Teach me to hear mermaids singing,   5
Or to keep off envy's stinging,
      And find
      What wind
Serves to advance an honest mind.

If thou be'st born to strange sights,   10
   Things invisible to see,
Ride ten thousand days and nights,
   Till age snow white hairs on thee.
Thou, when thou return'st, wilt tell me,
All strange wonders that befell thee,   15
      And swear,
      No where
Lives a woman true and fair.

If thou find'st one, let me know;
   Such a pilgrimage were sweet.   20
Yet do not, I would not go,
   Though at next door we might meet:
Though she were true when you met her,
And last till you write your letter,
      Yet she   25
      Will be
False, ere I come, to two or three.

2. *mandrake:* a plant with a pronged root like the legs of a man. When pulled up, popular superstition alleged it screamed.

All Kings, and all their favourites,
All glory of honours, beauties, wits,
The Sun itself, which makes times, as they pass,
Is elder by a year now than it was
5   When thou and I first one another saw.
All other things to their destruction draw,
    Only our love hath no decay;
This no to-morrow hath, nor yesterday;
Running it never runs from us away,
10 But truly keeps his first, last, everlasting day.

    Two graves must hide thine and my corse;
    If one might, death were no divorce.
Alas! as well as other princes, we
—Who prince enough in one another be—
15 Must leave at last in death these eyes and ears,
Oft fed with true oaths, and with sweet salt tears;
    But souls where nothing dwells but love
(All other thoughts being inmates) then shall prove
This, or a love increaséd there above,
20 When bodies to their graves, souls from their graves remove.

    And then we shall be throughly blest;
    But we no more than all the rest.
Here upon earth we're Kings, and none but we
Can be such Kings, nor of such subjects be.
25 Who is so safe as we? where none can do
Treason to us, except one of us two.
    True and false fears let us refrain,
Let us love nobly, and live, and add again
Years and years unto years, till we attain
30 To write threescore; this is the second of our reign.

18. *inmates:* boarders, intruders, not members of the family.
21. *throughly:* thoroughly, completely.

Where, like a pillow on a bed,
    A pregnant bank swell'd up, to rest
The violet's reclining head,
    Sat we two, one another's best.
Our hands were firmly cemented   5
    With a fast balm, which thence did spring;
Our eye-beams twisted, and did thread
    Our eyes upon one double string.
So to'entergraft our hands, as yet
    Was all the means to make us one;   10
And pictures in our eyes to get
    Was all our propagation.
As, 'twixt two equal armies, Fate
    Suspends uncertain victory,
Our souls (which to advance their state,   15
    Were gone out) hung 'twixt her and me.
And whilst our souls negotiate there,
    We like sepulchral statues lay;
All day, the same our postures were,
    And we said nothing, all the day.   20
If any, so by love refined,
    That he soul's language understood,
And by good love were grown all mind,
    Within convenient distance stood,
He (though he knew not which soul spake,   25
    Because both meant, both spake the same)
Might thence a new concoction take,
    And part far purer than he came.
This ecstacy doth unperplex
    (We said) and tell us what we love;   30
We see by this, it was not sex;
    We see, we saw not what did move:
But as all several souls contain
    Mixture of things they know not what,
Love these mix'd souls doth mix again,   35
    And makes both one, each this, and that.
A single violet transplant,

27. *concoction*: mixture, composition, quality, an alchemical term.

The strength, the colour, and the size,
(All which before was poor and scant)
40   Redoubles still, and multiplies.
When love with one another so
    Interinanimates two souls,
That abler soul, which thence doth flow,
    Defects of loneliness controls.
45 We, then, who are this new soul, know,
    Of what we are composed, and made,
For th' atomies of which we grow
    Are souls, whom no change can invade.
But O alas! so long, so far,
50   Our bodies why do we forbear?
They are ours, though they are not we; we are
    Th' intelligences, they the spheres.
We owe them thanks, because they thus
    Did us, to us, at first convey,
55 Yielded their forces, sense, to us,
    Nor are dross to us, but allay.
On man heaven's influence works not so,
    But that it first imprints the air;
So soul into the soul may flow,
60   Though it to body first repair.
As our blood labours to beget
    Spirits, as like souls as it can;
Because such fingers need to knit
    That subtle knot, which makes us man;
65 So must pure lovers' souls descend
    T'affections, and to faculties,
Which sense may reach and apprehend,
    Else a great prince in prison lies.
To'our bodies turn we then, that so

---

47. *atomies:* atoms out of which each individual is composed.

52. *intelligences . . . spheres:* the nine crystalline spheres of Ptolemaic astronomy of which the cosmos is constructed, each moved and guided by an Intelligence, or Angel.   56. *allay:* alloy.

61. *blood* and 62. *Spirits:* According to medieval physiology the animal spirits were rarified substances in the blood and were the medium through which the brain's commands were transmitted to the nerves and muscles and thus served as a link between soul and body.

63. *need:* are needed.

Weak men on love reveal'd may look;   70
Love's mysteries in souls do grow,
    But yet the body is his book.
And if some lover, such as we,
    Have heard this dialogue of one,
Let him still mark us, he shall see   75
    Small change when we're to bodies gone.

25 ⸙ *Holy Sonnets*

X

Death be not proud, though some have callèd thee
Mighty and dreadful, for thou art not so;
For those whom thou think'st thou dost overthrow
Die not, poor Death; nor yet canst thou kill me.
From rest and sleep, which but thy pictures be,   5
Much pleasure; then from thee much more must flow;
And soonest our best men with thee do go—
Rest of their bones and souls' delivery!
Thou'rt slave to Fate, Chance, kings, and desperate men,
And dost with poison, war, and sickness dwell;   10
And poppy or charms can make us sleep as well
And better than thy stroke. Why swell'st thou then?
One short sleep past, we wake eternally,
And Death shall be no more; Death, thou shalt die.

XIII

What if this present were the world's last night?
Mark in my heart, O Soul, where thou dost dwell,
The picture of Christ crucified, and tell
Whether that countenance can thee afright:
Tears in his eyes quench the amazing light,   5
Blood fills his frowns, which from his pierc'd head fell.
And can that tongue adjudge thee unto hell,
Which pray'd forgiveness for his foes' fierce spite?
No, no; but as in my idolatry

XIII, 9. *idolatry:* in my youthful sinful days when I made an idol of woman and worshipped Venus.

41

10   I said to all my profane mistresses,
       Beauty, of pity, foulness only is
       A sign of rigour: so I say to thee,
       To wicked spirits are horrid shapes assign'd,
       This beauteous form assures a piteous mind.

XIV

       Batter my heart, three-personed God; for you
       As yet but knock, breathe, shine, and seek to mend;
       That I may rise and stand, o'erthrow me and bend
       Your force to break, blow, burn and make me new.
5   I, like an usurped town, to another due,
       Labour to admit you, but Oh, to no end;
       Reason, your viceroy in me, me should defend,
       But is captived and proves weak or untrue.
       Yet dearly I love you and would be loved fain,
10   But am betrothed unto your enemy:
       Divorce me, untie or break that knot again,
       Take me to you, imprison me, for I
       Except you enthrall me, never shall be free,
       Nor ever chaste, except you ravish me.

BEN JONSON *1572-1637*

26 *1 The Triumph of Charis*

       See the Chariot at hand here of Love,
         Wherein my Lady rideth!
       Each that draws is a swan or a dove,
         And well the car Love guideth.
5   As she goes, all hearts do duty
         Unto her beauty;
       And enamour'd do wish, so they might
         But enjoy such a sight,

---

10. *profane mistresses:* in contrast to his present sacred mistress, *True Religion.*
11. *foulness:* ugliness.   12. *rigour:* sternness, hardness of heart, cruelty.
XIV, 8. *captived* is an iamb. The stress is on the second syllable.
  3. swans and doves were sacred to Venus.

That they still were to run by her side,
Thorough swords, thorough seas, whither she would ride.   10

Do but look on her eyes, they do light
  All that Love's world compriseth!
Do but look on her hair, it is bright
  As Love's star when it riseth!
Do but mark, her forehead's smoother   15
      Than words that soothe her;
And from her arch'd brows such a grace
      Sheds itself through the face,
As alone there triumphs to the life
All the gain, all the good, of the elements' strife.   20

Have you seen but a bright lily grow
  Before rude hands have touch'd it?
Have you mark'd but the fall of the snow
  Before the soil hath smutch'd it?
Have you felt the wool of beaver,   25
      Or swan's down ever?
Or have smelt of the bud of the brier,
      Or the nard in the fire?
Or have tasted the bag of the bee?
O so white, O so soft, O so sweet is she!   30

ROBERT HERRICK *1591-1674*

27 ⸗ *To the Virgins, to Make Much of Time*

        Gather ye rose-buds while ye may,
          Old Time is still a-flying:
        And this same flower that smiles today,
          Tomorrow will be dying.

20. *elements'*: earth, air, fire, and water, out of whose interaction all things are generated. Here Love or Venus is seen as the creative life force as in Lucretius' *De Rerum Natura*..

43

The glorious lamp of heaven, the Sun,
  The higher he's a-getting
The sooner will his race be run,
  And nearer he's to setting.

That age is best which is the first,
  When youth and blood are warmer;
But being spent, the worse, and worst
  Times, still succeed the former.

Then be not coy, but use your time;
  And while ye may, go marry:
For having lost but once your prime,
  You may for ever tarry.

28 ⸙ Upon Julia's Clothes

When as in silks my Julia goes
Then, then (methinks) how sweetly flows
That liquefaction of her clothes.

Next, when I cast mine eyes and see
That brave vibration each way free;
O how that glittering taketh me!

29 ⸙ To Daffodils

Fair Daffodils, we weep to see
  You haste away so soon:
As yet the early-rising Sun
  Has not attain'd his noon.
    Stay, stay,
  Until the hasting day
    Has run
  But to the even-song;
And, having pray'd together, we
  Will go with you along.

We have short time to stay, as you,
    We have as short a Spring!
As quick a growth to meet decay
    As you, or any thing.
        We die,   15
    As your hours do, and dry
        Away
    Like to the Summer's rain;
Or as the pearls of morning's dew
    Ne'er to be found again.   20

GEORGE HERBERT *1593-1633*

30 *The Collar*

I struck the board, and cry'd, No more;
    I will abroad!
What? shall I ever sigh and pine?
My lines and life are free; free as the road,
  Loose as the winde, as large as store,   5
    Shall I be still in suit?
  Have I no harvest but a thorn
  To let me blood, and not restore
What I have lost with cordial fruit?
    Sure there was wine   10
  Before my sighs did dry it: there was corn
    Before my tears did drown it.
  Is the year only lost to me?
    Have I no bays to crown it?
No flowers, no garlands gay? all blasted?   15
    All wasted?
  Not so, my heart: but there is fruit,
    And thou hast hands.
  Recover all thy sigh-blown age
On double pleasures: leave thy cold dispute   20
Of what is fit, and not; forsake thy cage,
    Thy rope of sands,

Which petty thoughts have made, and made to thee
    Good cable, to enforce and draw,
          And be thy law,
25
    While thou didst wink and wouldst not see.
          Away; take heed:
          I will abroad.
Call in thy death's head there: tie up thy fears.
30
          He that forbears
    To suit and serve his need,
          Deserves his load.
But as I rav'd and grew more fierce and wild
          At every word,
35
    Me thought I heard one calling, *Child;*
    And I replied, *My Lord*.

31 ⸰ *Love*

Love bade me welcome; yet my soul drew back,
    Guilty of dust and sin.
But quick-ey'd Love, observing me grow slack
    From my first entrance in,
5
Drew nearer to me, sweetly questioning
    If I lacked anything.

A guest, I answer'd, worthy to be here.
    Love said, You shall be he.
I, the unkind, ungrateful? Ah, my dear,
10
    I cannot look on Thee.
Love took my hand, and smiling, did reply,
    Who made the eyes but I?

Truth, Lord, but I have marred them: let my shame
    Go where it doth deserve.
15
And know you not, says Love, who bore the blame?
    My dear, then I will serve.
You must sit down, says Love, and taste my meat:
    So I did sit and eat.

Love: God.

46

When God at first made man,
Having a glass of blessings standing by—
Let us (said he) pour on him all we can;
Let the world's riches, which dispersed lie,
    Contract into a span.   5

So strength first made a way,
Then beauty flow'd, then wisdom, honour, pleasure:
When almost all was out, God made a stay,
Perceiving that, alone of all His treasure,
    Rest in the bottom lay.   10

For if I should (said he)
Bestow this jewel also on My creature,
He would adore My gifts instead of Me,
And rest in Nature, not the God of Nature:
    So both should losers be.   15

Yet let him keep the rest,
But keep them with repining restlessness;
Let him be rich and weary, that at least,
If goodness lead him not, yet weariness
    May toss him to My breast.   20

EDMUND WALLER *1606-1687*

33 ✦ *Go, Lovely Rose*

Go, lovely rose—
Tell her that wastes her time and me
That now she knows,
When I resemble her to thee,
How sweet and fair she seems to be.   5

Tell her that's young,
And shuns to have her graces spied,
That hadst thou sprung

In deserts where no men abide,
10   Thou must have uncommended died.

          Small is the worth
Of beauty from the light retired:
          Bid her come forth,
Suffer herself to be desired,
15   And not blush so to be admired.

          Then die—that she
The common fate of all things rare
          May read in thee:
How small a part of time they share
20   That are so wondrous sweet and fair.

JOHN MILTON   *1608-1674*

34 *1 At a Solemn Music*

      Blest pair of Sirens, pledges of Heav'n's joy,
      Sphere-born harmonious sisters, Voice and Verse,
      Wed your divine sounds, and mixt power employ,
      Dead things with inbreath'd sense able to pierce;
5   And to our high-rais'd phantasy present
      That undisturbéd song of pure concent,
      Aye sung before the sapphire-coloured throne
      To him that sits thereon
      With saintly shout and solemn jubilee;
10   Where the bright Seraphim in burning row
      Their loud uplifted angel trumpets blow,
      And the Cherubic host in thousand quires
      Touch their immortal harps of golden wires,
      With those just Spirits that wear victorious palms,

2. *Sphere-born:* music born of the motion of the nine crystalline spheres, those of the moon, sun and the planets surrounding the earth according to Ptolemaic astronomy.   6. *concent:* harmony.
7. *Aye:* everlastingly.   10. *Seraphim:* the highest of the nine orders of angels.
12. *Cherubic host:* the Cherubim, second highest order of angels.
14. *Spirits:* the martyrs, carrying palms symbolizing victory over death.

Hymns devout and holy psalms   15
Singing everlastingly:
That we on Earth, with undiscording voice,
May rightly answer that melodious noise;
As once we did, till disproportion'd sin
Jarr'd against nature's chime, and with harsh din   20
Broke the fair music that all creatures made
To their great Lord, whose love their motion sway'd
In perfect diapason, whilst they stood
In first obedience, and their state of good.
O may we soon again renew that song,   25
And keep in tune with Heaven, till God ere long
To his celestial consort us unite,
To live with him, and sing in endless morn of light.

35 ⸙ Lycidas

In this Monody the Author bewails a learned Friend,* unfortunately drowned in his passage from Chester on the Irish Seas, 1637; and, by occasion, foretells the ruin of our corrupted clergy, then in their height.

Yet once more, O ye laurels, and once more,
Ye myrtles brown, with ivy never sere,
I come to pluck your berries harsh and crude,
And with forced fingers rude
Shatter your leaves before the mellowing year.   5
Bitter constraint and sad occasion dear
Compels me to disturb your season due:
For Lycidas is dead, dead ere his prime,
Young Lycidas, and hath not left his peer.
Who would not sing for Lycidas? he knew   10
Himself to sing, and build the lofty rhyme.
He must not float upon his watery bier
Unwept, and welter to the parching wind,
Without the meed of some melodious tear.
Begin then, Sisters of the sacred well   15

19. *As once we did:* before Adam's fall destroyed man's harmony with nature
and with God.
* The learned friend was Edward King, a fellow student of Milton's at Cambridge,
who was drowned on August 10, 1637.
15. *Sisters of the sacred well:* the Muses.

That from beneath the seat of Jove doth spring;
Begin, and somewhat loudly sweep the string;
Hence with denial vain and coy excuse:
So may some gentle Muse
20   With lucky words favor *my* destined urn;
And as he passes, turn
And bid fair peace be to my sable shroud.
    For we were nursed upon the self-same hill,
Fed the same flock by fountain, shade, and rill.
25   Together both, ere the high lawns appeared
Under the opening eye-lids of the Morn,
We drove a-field, and both together heard
What time the gray-fly winds her sultry horn,
Battening our flocks with the fresh dews of night;
30   Oft till the star, that rose at evening bright,
Toward heaven's descent had sloped his westering wheel.
Meanwhile the rural ditties were not mute;
Tempered to the oaten flute,
Rough Satyrs danced, and Fauns with cloven heel
35   From the glad sound would not be absent long;
And old Damoetas loved to hear our song.
    But, O! the heavy change, now thou art gone,
Now thou art gone, and never must return!
Thee, Shepherd, thee the woods and desert caves,
40   With wild thyme and the gadding vine o'ergrown,
And all their echoes, mourn:
The willows and the hazel copses green
Shall now no more be seen
Fanning their joyous leaves to thy soft lays.
45   As killing as the canker to the rose,
Or taint-worm to the weanling herds that graze,
Or frost to flowers, that their gay wardrobe wear
When first the white-thorn blows;
Such, Lycidas, thy loss to shepherd's ear.
50   Where were ye, Nymphs, when the remorseless deep
Closed o'er the head of your loved Lycidas?
For neither were ye playing on the steep

23. *nursed upon the self-same hill:* educated at the same university.
28. *What time:* when.   50. *Nymphs:* female spirits, guardians of the ocean.

Where your old bards, the famous Druids, lie,
Nor on the shaggy top of Mona high,
Nor yet where Deva spreads her wizard stream.   55
Ay me! I fondly dream
"Had ye been there,"—for what could that have done?
What could the Muse herself that Orpheus bore,
The Muse herself, for her enchanting son,
Whom universal nature did lament,   60
When by the rout that made the hideous roar
His gory visage down the stream was sent,
Down the swift Hebrus to the Lesbian shore?
    Alas! what boots it with uncessant care
To tend the homely, slighted, shepherd's trade   65
And strictly meditate the thankless Muse?
Were it not better done, as others use,
To sport with Amaryllis in the shade,
Or with the tangles of Neaera's hair?
Fame is the spur that the clear spirit doth raise   70
(That last infirmity of noble mind)
To scorn delights, and live laborious days;
But the fair guerdon when we hope to find,
And think to burst out into sudden blaze,
Comes the blind Fury with the abhorred shears   75
And slits the thin-spun life. "But not the praise,"
Phoebus replied, and touched my trembling ears:
"Fame is no plant that grows on mortal soil,
Nor in the glistering foil
Set off to the world, nor in broad rumor lies: 80
But lives and spreads aloft by those pure eyes
And perfect witness of all-judging Jove;
As he pronounces lastly on each deed,
Of so much fame in heaven expect thy meed."

54. *Mona:* Roman name of the island of Anglesy, near where Edward King was
lost.   55. *Deva:* the river Dee which flows into the Irish Sea.
56. *fondly:* foolishly, too hopefully.
58. *Muse:* Calliope, the Muse of Epic Poetry, was the mother of Orpheus.
64. *what boots it:* of what avail is it.
65. *shepherd's trade:* the poet and scholar's vocation.
77. *Phoebus:* Apollo, the god of poetry.
82. *Jove:* God in the Christian rather than the pagan sense.

85   O fountain Arethuse, and thou honored flood.
        Smooth-sliding Mincius, crowned with vocal reeds,
        That strain I heard was of a higher mood.
        But now my oat proceeds,
        And listens to the herald of the sea
90   That came in Neptune's plea;
        He asked the waves, and asked the felon winds,
        What hard mishap hath doomed this gentle swain?
        And questioned every gust of rugged wings
        That blows from off each beaked promontory:
95   They knew not of his story;
        And sage Hippotades their answer brings,
        That not a blast was from his dungeon strayed;
        The air was calm, and on the level brine
        Sleek Panope with all her sisters played.
100   It was that fatal and perfidious bark,
        Built in the eclipse, and rigged with curses dark,
        That sunk so low that sacred head of thine.
           Next Camus, reverend sire, went footing slow,
        His mantle hairy, and his bonnet sedge,
105   Inwrought with figures dim, and on the edge
        Like to that sanguine flower inscribed with woe.
        "Ah! who hath reft," quoth he, "my dearest pledge?"
        Last came, and last did go
        The Pilot of the Galilean lake;
110   Two massy keys he bore of metals twain
        (The golden opes, the iron shuts amain);
        He shook his mitred locks, and stern bespake:
        "How well could I have spared for thee, young swain,
        Enow of such, as for their bellies' sake
115   Creep and intrude and climb into the fold!
        Of other care they little reckoning make

85. *Arethuse:* a spring in Sicily associated with Theocritus, the father of pastoral poetry.
86. *Mincius:* a river in Tuscany, associated with Virgil.
89. *herald of the sea:* Triton, who came to present the sea-god Neptune's plea of innocence in the drowning of Lycidas.
96. *Hippotades:* Aeolus, god of the winds.
99. *Panope:* one of the fifty Nereids, or sea-nymphs.
103. *Camus:* a personification of the river Cam, which flows through Cambridge.
109. *Pilot of the Galilean lake:* St. Peter.

52

Than how to scramble at the shearers' feast,
And shove away the worthy bidden guest.
Blind mouths! that scarce themselves know how to hold
A sheep-hook, or have learned aught else the least   120
That to the faithful herdman's art belongs!
What recks it them? What need they? They are sped;
And when they list, their lean and flashy songs
Grate on their scrannel pipes of wretched straw;
The hungry sheep look up, and are not fed,   125
But, swol'n with wind and the rank mist they draw,
Rot inwardly, and foul contagion spread:
Besides what the grim wolf with privy paw
Daily devours apace, and nothing said:
—But that two-handed engine at the door   130
Stands ready to smite once, and smite no more."
     Return, Alpheus; the dread voice is past
That shrunk thy streams; return, Sicilian Muse,
And call the vales, and bid them hither cast
Their bells and flowerets of a thousand hues.   135
Ye valleys low, where the mild whispers use
Of shades, and wanton winds, and gushing brooks
On whose fresh lap the swart star sparely looks;
Throw hither all your quaint enameled eyes
That on the green turf suck the honeyed showers,   140
And purple all the ground with vernal flowers.
Bring the rathe primrose that forsaken dies,
The tufted crow-toe, and pale jessamine,
The white pink, and the pansy freaked with jet,
The glowing violet,   145
The musk-rose, and the well-attired woodbine,

119. *Blind mouths:* unworthy priests, pastors, or bishops; they ought to lead their
     flock, but are blind; they ought to feed their flock, but are nothing but
     mouths that feed themselves. A striking oxymoron.
120. *sheep-hook:* a bishop's symbolic crook.   121. *herdsman:* pastor or bishop.
122. *sped:* They have got what they wanted.
124. *scrannel:* weak, shrill, harsh, feeble sounding.
128. *wolf:* the Roman Catholic Church.
130. *two-handed engine:* probably, though not certainly, the headsman's axe.
132. *Alpheus:* a river of Sicily associated with Theocritus and thus with pastoral
     poetry, whose Muse is evoked in the next line to announce a return from
     the harsh digression to the softer pastoral strain.

With cowslips wan that hang the pensive head,
And every flower that sad embroidery wears;
Bid amaranthus all his beauty shed,
150 And daffadillies fill their cups with tears
To strew the laureate hearse where Lycid lies.
For so to interpose a little ease,
Let our frail thoughts dally with false surmise.
Ay me! whilst thee the shores and sounding seas
155 Wash far away, where'er thy bones are hurled;
Whether beyond the stormy Hebrides
Where thou, perhaps, under the whelming tide,
Visit'st the bottom of the monstrous world;
Or whether thou, to our moist vows denied,
160 Sleep'st by the fable of Bellerus old,
Where the great Vision of the guarded mount
Looks toward Namancos and Bayona's hold.
Look homeward, Angel, now, and melt with ruth:
And, O ye dolphins, waft the hapless youth!
165   Weep no more, woeful shepherds, weep no more,
For Lycidas, your sorrow, is not dead,
Sunk though he be beneath the watery floor;
So sinks the day-star in the ocean bed,
And yet anon repairs his drooping head,
170 And tricks his beams, and with new-spangled ore
Flames in the forehead of the morning sky:
So Lycidas sunk low, but mounted high
Through the dear might of Him that walked the waves;
Where, other groves and other streams along,
175 With nectar pure his oozy locks he laves,
And hears the unexpressive nuptial song
In the blest kingdoms meek of joy and love.
There entertain him all the saints above
In solemn troops, and sweet societies,
180 That sing, and singing in their glory move,
And wipe the tears for ever from his eyes.

160. *Bellerus:* a fabulous hero associated with Land's End in Cornwall.
161. *guarded mount:* St. Michael's Mount in Cornwall, supposed to be under the protection of the Archangel.
162. *Namancos and Bayona's hold:* two strongholds in Spain.
176. *unexpressive:* inexpressible.

Now, Lycidas, the shepherds weep no more;
Henceforth thou art the Genius of the shore
In thy large recompense, and shalt be good
To all that wander in that perilous flood.   185
    Thus sang the uncouth swain to the oaks and rills,
While the still morn went out with sandals gray;
He touched the tender stops of various quills,
With eager thought warbling his Doric lay:
And now the sun had stretched out all the hills,   190
And now was dropt into the western bay.
At last he rose, and twitched his mantle blue:
Tomorrow to fresh woods, and pastures new.

36 ⁊ Hail, Holy Light

FROM *Paradise Lost*

Hail holy Light, offspring of Heav'n first-born,
Or of th' Eternal Coeternal beam
May I express thee unblam'd? since God is Light,
And never but in unapproached Light
Dwelt from Eternity, dwelt then in thee,   5
Bright effluence of bright essence increate.
Or hearest thou rather pure Ethereal stream,
Whose Fountain who shall tell? before the Sun,
Before the Heavens thou wert, and at the voice
Of God, as with a Mantle didst invest   10
The rising world of water dark and deep,
Won from the void and formless infinite.
Thee I re-visit now with bolder wing,
Escaped the *Stygian* Pool, though long detained
In that obscure sojourn, while in my flight   15
    Through utter and through middle darkness borne

183. *Genius of the shore:* guardian spirit of the coast.
186. *uncouth swain:* the poet Milton, as yet unknown.
189. *Doric:* the rustic dialect in which the Sicilian pastoral poets wrote.
   6. *increate:* uncreated; self-existent.
  14. *the Stygian Pool:* the river Styx surrounding Hell.
  16. *utter and middle darkness:* Hell and Chaos.

With other notes then to th' *Orphean* Lyre
I sung of *Chaos* and *Eternal Night,*
Taught by the heavenly Muse to venture down
20 The dark descent, and up to reascend,
Though hard and rare: thee I revisit safe,
And feel thy sovereign vital Lamp; but thou
Revisit'st not these eyes, that roll in vain
To find thy piercing ray, and find no dawn;
25 So thick a drop serene hath quenched their Orbs,
Or dim suffusion veiled. Yet not the more
Cease I to wander where the Muses haunt
Clear Spring, or shady Grove, or Sunny Hill,
Smit with the love of sacred song; but chief
30 Thee *Zion* and the flowery Brooks beneath
That wash thy hallowed feet, and warbling flow,
Nightly I visit: nor sometimes forget
Those other two equalled with me in Fate,
So were I equalled with them in renown,
35 Blind *Thamyris* and blind *Mæonides,*
And *Tiresias* and *Phineus* Prophets old.
Then feed on thoughts, that voluntary move
Harmonious numbers; as the wakeful Bird
Sings darkling, and in shadiest Covert hid
40 Tunes her nocturnal Note. Thus with the Year
Seasons return, but not to me returns
Day, or the sweet approach of Even or Morn,
Or sight of vernal bloom, or Summer's Rose,
Or flocks, or herds, or human face divine;
45 But cloud instead, and ever-during dark
Surrounds me, from the cheerful ways of men
Cut off, and for the Book of knowledge fair

17. *Orphean Lyre:* in secular not in sacred verse because writing of hell. This is
in contrast to heavenly Muse of line 19.
25. *serene: gutta serena,* Latin medical term for blindness where the eye retains
a normal appearance.
35. *Thamyris:* a legendary poet mentioned by Homer as being blind.
Mæonides: Homer.
36. *Tiresias:* the blind prophet in Oedipus by Sophocles.
Phineus: a Thracian soothsayer blinded by the Sun-god.
38. *Harmonious numbers:* musical verses.
wakeful Bird: the nightingale.

Presented with a Universal blank
Of Nature's works to me expung'd and raised,
And wisdom at one entrance quite shut out.   50
So much the rather thou Celestial Light
Shine inward, and the mind through all her powers
Irradiate, there plant eyes, all mist from thence
Purge and disperse, that I may see and tell
Of things invisible to mortal sight.   55

37 ⟡ How Soon Hath Time

How soon hath Time, the subtle thief of youth,
    Stol'n on his wing my three-and-twentieth year!
    My hasting days fly on with full career,
    But my late spring no bud or blossom shew'th.
Perhaps my semblance might deceive the truth,   5
    That I to manhood am arriv'd so near,
    And inward ripeness doth much less appear,
    That some more timely-happy spirits indu'th.
Yet it be less or more, or soon or slow,
    It shall be still in strictest measure ev'n,   10
    To that same lot, however mean or high,
Toward which Time leads me, and the will of Heav'n;
    All is, if I have grace to use it so,
    As ever in my great Taskmaster's eye.

38 ⟡ On His Deceased Wife

Methought I saw my late espousèd Saint
    Brought to me like *Alcestis* from the grave,
    Whom *Jove's* great son to her glad husband gave,
    Rescu'd from death by force though pale and faint
Mine as whom washt from spot of child-bed taint,   5

49. *raised*: erased.

On His Deceased Wife—Though long thought to have been written on the death of Milton's second wife, Catherine Woodcock, who died in childbed February, 1658, recent scholarship seems to show it was more likely written about his first wife, Mary Powell.

Purification in the old Law did save,
And such, as yet once more I trust to have
Full sight of her in Heaven without restraint,
Came vested all in white, pure as her mind:
10   Her face was veil'd, yet to my fancied sight,
Love, sweetness, goodness, in her person shin'd
So clear, as in no face with more delight.
But O as to embrace me she enclin'd
I wak'd, she fled, and day brought back my night.

ANDREW MARVELL *1621-1678*

39 ⟡ *To His Coy Mistress*

Had we but world enough, and time,
This coyness, lady, were no crime.
We would sit down, and think which way
To walk, and pass our long love's day.
5   Thou by the Indian Ganges' side
Should'st rubies find: I by the tide
Of Humber would complain. I would
Love you ten years before the Flood,
And you should, if you please, refuse
10   Till the conversion of the Jews.
My vegetable love should grow
Vaster than empires, and more slow.
An hundred years should go to praise
Thine eyes, and on thy forehead gaze:
15   Two hundred to adore each breast:
But thirty thousand to the rest;
An age at least to every part,
And the last age should show your heart.
For, lady, you deserve this state,
20   Nor would I love at lower rate.
But at my back I always hear

Coy: modest, reserved, chaste.
    7. *Humber:* river flowing through Marvell's native town, Hull.
    11. *vegetable:* without blood or animal vigor.

Time's wingéd chariot hurrying near:
And yonder all before us lie
Deserts of vast eternity.
Thy beauty shall no more be found;   25
Nor, in thy marble vault, shall sound
My echoing song: then worms shall try
That long-preserved virginity,
And your quaint honor turn to dust,
And into ashes all my lust.   30
The grave's a fine and private place,
But none, I think, do there embrace.
    Now, therefore, while the youthful hue
Sits on thy skin like morning dew,
And while thy willing soul transpires   35
At every pore with instant fires,
Now let us sport us while we may;
And now, like amorous birds of prey,
Rather at once our Time devour,
Than languish in his slow-chapt power.   40
Let us roll all our strength and all
Our sweetness up into one ball,
And tear our pleasures with rough strife
Thorough the iron gates of life.
Thus, though we cannot make our sun   45
Stand still, yet we will make him run.

40 ⁊ The Garden

How vainly men themselves amaze
To win the palm, the oak, or bays;
And their incessant labors see
Crowned from some single herb, or tree,
Whose short and narrow-vergéd shade   5
Does prudently their toils upbraid;
While all flowers and all trees do close
To weave the garlands of repose!

40. *slow-chapt:* slow-jawed, slowly chewing.
44. *Thorough:* through.   7. *close:* unite.

Fair Quiet, have I found thee here,
10   And Innocence, thy sister dear!
Mistaken long, I sought you then
In busy companies of men.
Your sacred plants, if here below,
Only among the plants will grow;
15   Society is all but rude
To this delicious solitude.

No white nor red was ever seen
So amorous as this lovely green.
Fond lovers, cruel as their flame,
20   Cut in these trees their mistress' name:
Little, alas! they know or heed
How far these beauties hers exceed!
Fair trees! wheres'e'er your barks I wound
No name shall but your own be found.

25   When we have run our passion's heat,
Love hither makes his best retreat.
The gods, that mortal beauty chase,
Still in a tree did end their race;
Apollo hunted Daphne so,
30   Only that she might laurel grow;
And Pan did after Syrinx speed,
Not as a nymph, but for a reed.

What wondrous life is this I lead!
Ripe apples drop about my head;
35   The luscious clusters of the vine
Upon my mouth do crush their wine;
The nectarine, and curious peach,
Into my hands themselves do reach;
Stumbling on melons, as I pass,
40   Ensnared with flowers, I fall on grass.

16. *To:* compared to.   37. *curious:* exquisite.

Meanwhile, the mind, from pleasure less,
Withdraws into its happiness:
The mind, that ocean where each kind
Does straight its own resemblance find;
Yet it creates, transcending these,   45
Far other worlds, and other seas;
Annihilating all that's made
To a green thought in a green shade.

Here at the fountain's sliding foot,
Or at some fruit-tree's mossy root,   50
Casting the body's vest aside,
My soul into the boughs does glide:
There like a bird it sits, and sings,
Then whets and combs its silver wings;
And, till prepared for longer flight,   55
Waves in its plumes the various light.

Such was that happy garden-state,
While man there walked without a mate:
After a place so pure and sweet,
What other help could yet be meet?   60
But 'twas beyond a mortal's share
To wander solitary there:
Two Paradises 'twere in one,
To live in Paradise alone.

How well the skillful gardener drew   65
Of flowers, and herbs, this dial new!
Where, from above, the milder sun
Does through a fragrant zodiac run;
And, as it works, the industrious bee
Computes its time as well as we.   70
How could such sweet and wholesome hours
Be reckoned but with herbs and flowers!

54. *whets:* preens.

41 ⁊ *The World*

I saw Eternity the other night,
Like a great Ring of pure and endless light,
   All calm, as it was bright;
And round beneath it, Time in hours, days, years,
5   Driven by the spheres,
Like a vast shadow moved: in which the world
   And all her train were hurled.
The doting lover in his quaintest strain
   Did there complain;
10 Near him, his lute, his fancy, and his flights,
   Wit's sour delights,
With gloves, and knots, the silly snares of pleasure,
   Yet his dear treasure,
All scattered lay, while he his eyes did pore
15   Upon a flower.

The darksome statesman, hung with weights and woe,
Like a thick midnight-fog, moved there so slow,
   He did not stay, nor go;
Condemning thoughts—like sad eclipses—scowl
20   Upon his soul,
And clouds of crying witnesses without
   Pursued him with one shout.
Yet digged the mole, and lest his ways be found,
   Worked under ground,
25 Where he did clutch his prey; but one did see
   That policy;
Churches and altars fed him; perjuries
   Were gnats and flies;
It rained about him blood and tears; but he
30   Drank them as free.

8. *quaintest strain;* conventional, artificial, elegant and courtly love poetry.
11. *Wit:* worldly cleverness.
16. *darksome statesman:* secretive Machiavellian politician.   25. *one:* God.
30. *as free:* freely, liberally, generously, copiously, and without harm to himself.

The fearful miser on a heap of rust
Sate pining all his life there, did scarce trust
   His own hands with the dust,
Yet would not place one piece above, but lives
   In fear of thieves.   35
Thousands there were as frantic as himself
   And hugged each one his pelf;
The downright epicure placed heaven in sense,
   And scorned pretence;
While others, slipped into a wide excess,   40
   Said little less;
The weaker sort slight, trivial wares enslave,
   Who think them brave;
   And poor, despiséd Truth sat counting by
   Their victory.   45

Yet some, who all this while did weep and sing,
And sing, and weep, soared up into the Ring;
   But most would use no wing.
O fools (said I) thus to prefer dark night
   Before true light!   50
To live in grots and caves, and hate the day
   Because it shows the way,
The way, which from this dead and dark abode
   Leads up to God,
A way where you might tread the sun, and be   55
   More bright than he.
But as I did their madness so discuss,
   One whispered thus,
"This Ring the Bridegroom did for none provide,
   But for His bride."

John, Cap. 2, Ver. 16, 17.

31. *fearful:* full of fear.   33. *dust:* gold.
38. *sense:* sensation, sensuous pleasure.
39. *scorned pretence:* affected to be forthright and honest in his rejection of spiritual values.   44. *counting:* observing, taking note.
59. *Bridegroom:* See *Revelations* 21:9.

42 ⸍ *A Song for St. Cecilia's Day*

NOVEMBER 22, 1687

1.

From harmony, from heavenly harmony,
    This universal frame began:
    When nature underneath a heap
      Of jarring atoms lay,
5   And could not heave her head,
The tuneful voice was heard from high,
      Arise, ye more than dead!
Then cold, and hot, and moist, and dry,
    In order to their stations leap,
10   And Music's power obey.
From harmony, from heavenly harmony,
    This universal frame began:
    From harmony to harmony
Through all the compass of the notes it ran,
15   The diapason closing full in Man.

2.

What passion cannot Music raise and quell?
    When Jubal struck the corded shell,

St. Cecilia's Day: November 22 when an annual concert was held in London. Cecilia was the patron saint of music, the reputed inventor of the pipe organ.

  1. *From harmony:* A Platonic doctrine but see also Job XXXVIII, 1-7 and Milton, At a Solemn Music, p. 48.

  4. *jarring atoms:* this atomic theory of the creation of the universe derives from the Epicurean philosophers.

  8. *cold, hot, moist, dry:* the qualities of the four elements—air, fire, water, and earth.

17. *Jubal:* "the father of all such as handle the harp and organ," Gen. IV, 21.

His listening brethren stood around,
    And, wondering, on their faces fell
To worship that celestial sound: 20
Less than a God they thought there could not dwell
    Within the hollow of that shell,
    That spoke so sweetly, and so well.
What passion cannot Music raise and quell?

3.

The trumpet's loud clangour   25
    Excites us to arms,
With shrill notes of anger,
    And mortal alarms.
The double double double beat
    Of the thundering drum   30
    Cries Hark! the foes come;
Charge, charge, 'tis too late to retreat!

4.

The soft complaining flute,
In dying notes, discovers
The woes of hopeless lovers,   35
Whose dirge is whisper'd by the warbling lute.

5.

Sharp violins proclaim
Their jealous pangs and desperation,
Fury, frantic indignation,
Depth of pains, and height of passion,   40
    For the fair, disdainful dame.

6.

But O, what art can teach,
What human voice can reach,
    The sacred organ's praise?
Notes inspiring holy love,   45
Notes that wing their heavenly ways
    To mend the choirs above.

65

7

Orpheus could lead the savage race;
And trees unrooted left their place,
50   Sequacious of the lyre;
But bright Cecilia rais'd the wonder higher:
When to her organ vocal breath was given,
An angel heard, and straight appear'd
Mistaking Earth for Heaven.

GRAND CHORUS

55 As from the power of sacred lays
    The spheres began to move,
And sung the great Creator's praise
    To all the Blest above;
So when the last and dreadful hour
60 This crumbling pageant shall devour,
The trumpet shall be heard on high,
The dead shall live, the living die,
And Music shall untune the sky!

43 *To the Memory of Mr. Oldham*

Farewell, too little and too lately known,
Whom I began to think and call my own:
For sure our souls were near allied, and thine
Cast in the same poetic mold with mine.
5 One common note on either lyre did strike,
And knaves and fools we both abhorred alike.
To the same goal did both our studies drive:
The last set out the soonest did arrive.
Thus Nisus fell upon the slippery place,
10 Whilst his young friend performed and won the race.

50. *Sequacious:* following or submitting to.
60. *crumbling pageant:* human history brought to an end by the Trumpet of
Gabriel sounding the call to the Last Judgment.
Mr. Oldham: The poet and satirist John Oldham died at the age of thirty in 1683.
9. *Nisus:* In Virgil's *Aeneid* V:327 ff. it is told how Nisus slipping on the spot
where bullocks had been sacrificed threw himself in front of a rival and
thus aided his friend Euryalus to win.

O early ripe! to thy abundant store
What could advancing age have added more?
It might (what nature never gives the young)
Have taught the numbers of thy native tongue.
But satire needs not those, and wit will shine   15
Through the harsh cadence of a rugged line.
A noble error, and but seldom made,
When poets are by too much force betray'd.
Thy generous fruits, though gathered ere their prime,
Still showed a quickness; and maturing time   20
But mellows what we write to the dull sweets of rhyme.
Once more, hail, and farewell! farewell, thou young,
But ah! too short, Marcellus of our tongue!
Thy brows with ivy and with laurels bound;
But Fate and gloomy night encompass thee around.   25

ALEXANDER POPE   *1688-1744*

44 ' *Ode on Solitude*

    Happy the man whose wish and care
        A few paternal acres bound,
    Content to breathe his native air,
            In his own ground.

    Whose herds with milk, whose fields with bread,   5
        Whose flocks supply him with attire,
    Whose trees in summer yield him shade,
            In winter fire.

    Blest, who can unconcern'dly find
        Hours, days, and years slide soft away,   10
    In health of body, peace of mind,
            Quiet by day,

    Sound sleep by night; study and ease,
        Together mix'd; sweet recreation;

23. *Marcellus:* young nephew and heir of Augustus, mourned by Virgil.

67

And Innocence, which most does please
With meditation.

Thus let me live, unseen, unknown,
Thus unlamented let me die,
Steal from the world, and not a stone
20   Tell where I lie.

45 ♪ To a Young Lady: On Her Leaving the Town After the Coronation

As some fond Virgin, whom her mother's care
Drags from the Town to wholesome Country air,
Just when she learns to roll a melting eye,
And hear a spark, yet think no danger nigh;
5 From the dear man unwilling she must sever,
Yet takes one kiss before she parts forever:
Thus from the world fair Zephalinda flew,
Saw others happy, and with sighs withdrew;
Not that their pleasures caus'd her discontent,
10 She sigh'd not that they stay'd, but that she went.
   She went, to plain-work and to purling brooks,
Old-fashion'd halls, dull Aunts, and croaking rooks:
She went from op'ra, park, assembly, play,
To morning walks, and pray'rs three hours a day;
15 To pass her time 'twixt reading and bohea,
To muse, and spill her solitary tea,
Or o'er cold coffee trifle with the spoon,
Count the slow clock, and dine exact at noon;
Divert her eyes with pictures in the fire,
20 Hum half a tune, tell stories to the squire;
Up to her godly garret after sev'n,
There starve and pray, for that's the way to heav'n.

To a Young Lady: Though originally written for Teresa Blount, Pope later changed the title to address it to her younger sister and one of his closest friends, Martha Blount. The coronation was that of George the First, October 20, 1714.

7. *Zephalinda:* a fanciful name used by Teresa Blount in a 'fantastic' corre-spondence with a family friend.   11. *plain-work:* crochet.
15. *bohea:* an expensive Chinese black tea.

Some Squire, perhaps, you take delight to rack;
Whose game is Whisk, whose treat a toast in sack;
Who visits with a gun, presents you birds,   25
Then gives a smacking buss, and cries,—No words!
Or with his hound comes hollowing from the stable,
Makes love with nods, and knees beneath a table;
Whose laughs are hearty, tho' his jests are coarse,
And loves you best of all things—but his horse.   30

   In some fair ev'ning, on your elbow laid,
You dream of Triumphs in the rural shade;
In pensive thought recall the fancy'd scene,
See Coronations rise on ev'ry green;
Before you pass th' imaginary sights   35
Of Lords, and Earls, and Dukes, and garter'd Knights,
While the spread fan o'ershades your closing eyes;
Then give one flirt, and all the vision flies.
Thus vanish sceptres, coronets, and balls,
And leave you in lone woods, or empty walls.   40

   So when your Slave, at some dear idle time,
(Not plagu'd with head-aches, or the want of rhyme)
Stands in the streets, abstracted from the crew,
And while he seems to study, thinks of you;
Just when his fancy points your sprightly eyes,   45
Or sees the blush of Parthenissa rise,
Gay pats my shoulder, and you vanish quite;
Streets, Chairs, and Coxcombs rush upon my sight;
Vex'd to be still in town, I knit my brow,
Look sour, and hum a tune—as you may now.   50

46 ∕ Elegy to the Memory of an Unfortunate Lady

   What beck'ning ghost, along the moonlight shade
Invites my steps, and points to yonder glade?
'Tis she!—but why that bleeding bosom gor'd,

---

24. *Whisk:* an old form of Whist, a card game like Bridge in which trumps are decided by chance.   32. *Triumphs:* fêtes, parades, spectacles.
41. *your Slave:* the poet himself, speaking gallantly and not quite seriously.
46. *Parthenissa:* name used by Teresa's younger sister Martha, Pope's devoted lifelong friend.   48. *Chairs:* sedan-chairs.

Why dimly gleams the visionary sword?
Oh ever beauteous, ever friendly! tell,
Is it, in heav'n, a crime to love too well?
To bear too tender, or too firm a heart,
To act a Lover's, or a Roman's part?
Is there no bright reversion in the sky,
For those who greatly think, or bravely die?

   Why bade ye else, ye Pow'rs! her soul aspire
Above the vulgar flight of low desire?
Ambition first sprung from your blest abodes;
The glorious fault of Angels and of Gods;
Thence to their Images on earth it flows,
And in the breasts of Kings and Heroes glows!
Most souls, 'tis true, but peep out once an age,
Dull sullen pris'ners in the body's cage:
Dim lights of life, that burn a length of years,
Useless, unseen, as lamps in sepulchres;
Like Eastern Kings, a lazy state they keep,
And close confin'd to their own palace, sleep.

   From these perhaps (ere nature bade her die)
Fate snatch'd her early to the pitying sky.
As into air the purer spirits flow,
And sep'rate from their kindred dregs below;
So flew the soul to its congenial place,
Nor left one virtue to redeem her Race.

   But thou, false guardian of a charge too good,
Thou, mean deserter of thy brother's blood!
See on these ruby lips the trembling breath,
These cheeks now fading at the blast of death:
Cold is that breast which warm'd the world before,
And those love-darting eyes must roll no more.

   Thus, if Eternal justice rules the ball,
Thus shall your wives, and thus your children fall;
On all the line a sudden vengeance waits,
And frequent herses shall besiege your gates.
There passengers shall stand, and pointing say,

5

10

15

20

25

30

35

---

8. *To act . . . a Roman's part:* to commit suicide.
25-26. *As into air,* etc.: the image is of chemical distillation.
  29. *false guardian:* the Lady's guardian and uncle, whose hardness of heart is
alleged to be responsible for her death.

(While the long fun'rals blacken all the way)   40
"Lo these were they, whose souls the Furies steel'd,
And curs'd with hearts unknowing how to yield."
Thus unlamented pass the proud away,
The gaze of fools, and pageant of a day!
So perish all, whose breast ne'er learn'd to glow   45
For others' good, or melt at others' woe.
    What can atone (oh ever-injur'd shade!)
Thy fate unpity'd, and thy rites unpaid?
No friend's complaint, no kind domestic tear
Pleas'd thy pale ghost, or grac'd thy mournful bier.   50
By foreign hands thy dying eyes were clos'd,
By foreign hands thy decent limbs compos'd,
By foreign hands thy humble grave adorn'd,
By strangers honour'd, and by strangers mourn'd!
What tho' no friends in sable weeds appear,   55
Grieve for an hour, perhaps, then mourn a year,
And bear about the mockery of woe
To midnight dances, and the public show?
What tho' no weeping Loves thy ashes grace,
Nor polish'd marble emulate thy face?   60
What tho' no sacred earth allow thee room,
Nor hallow'd dirge be mutter'd o'er thy tomb?
Yet shall thy grave with rising flow'rs be drest,
And the green turf lie lightly on thy breast:
There shall the morn her earliest tears bestow,   65
There the first roses of the year shall blow;
While Angels with their silver wings o'ershade
The ground, now sacred by thy reliques made.
    So peaceful rests, without a stone, a name,
What once had beauty, titles, wealth, and fame.   70
How lov'd, how honour'd once, avails thee not,
To whom related, or by whom begot;
A heap of dust alone remains of thee,
'Tis all thou art, and all the proud shall be!
    Poets themselves must fall, like those they sung,   75
Deaf the prais'd ear, and mute the tuneful tongue.
Ev'n he, whose soul now melts in mournful lays,
Shall shortly want the gen'rous tear he pays;
Then from his closing eyes thy form shall part,

And the last pang shall tear thee from his heart,
        Life's idle business at one gasp be o'er,
        The Muse forgot, and thou be lov'd no more!

                    THOMAS GRAY *1716-1771*

47 *Elegy Written in a Country Churchyard*

        The Curfew tolls the knell of parting day,
            The lowing herd wind slowly o'er the lea,
        The plowman homeward plods his weary way,
            And leaves the world to darkness and to me.

5   Now fades the glimmering landscape on the sight,
            And all the air a solemn stillness holds,
        Save where the beetle wheels his droning flight,
            And drowsy tinklings lull the distant folds;

        Save that from yonder ivy-mantled tower
10   The moping owl does to the moon complain
        Of such as wandering near her secret bower
            Molest her ancient solitary reign.

        Beneath those rugged elms, that yew-tree's shade,
            Where heaves the turf in many a mouldering heap,
15   Each in his narrow cell for ever laid,
            The rude Forefathers of the hamlet sleep.

        The breezy call of incense-breathing Morn,
            The swallow twittering from the straw-built shed,
        The cock's shrill clarion, or the echoing horn,
20   No more shall rouse them from their lowly bed.

        For them no more the blazing hearth shall burn,
            Or busy housewife ply her evening care:
        No children run to lisp their sire's return,
            Or climb his knees the envied kiss to share.

Oft did the harvest to their sickle yield,   25
   Their furrow oft the stubborn glebe has broke;
How jocund did they drive their team afield!
   How bowed the woods beneath their sturdy stroke!

Let not Ambition mock their useful toil,
   Their homely joys, and destiny obscure;   30
Nor Grandeur hear with a disdainful smile
   The short and simple annals of the poor.

The boast of heraldry, the pomp of power,
   And all that beauty, all that wealth e'er gave,
Awaits alike the inevitable hour.   35
   The paths of glory lead but to the grave.

Nor you, ye Proud, impute to these the fault,
   If Memory o'er their Tomb no Trophies raise,
Where through the long-drawn aisle and fretted vault
   The pealing anthem swells the note of praise.   40

Can storied urn or animated bust
   Back to its mansion call the fleeting breath?
Can Honor's voice provoke the silent dust,
   Or Flattery sooth the dull cold ear of Death?

Perhaps in this neglected spot is laid   45
   Some heart once pregnant with celestial fire;
Hands, that the rod of empire might have swayed,
   Or waked to ecstasy the living lyre.

But Knowledge to their eyes her ample page
   Rich with the spoils of time did ne'er unroll;   50
Chill Penury repressed their noble rage,
   And froze the genial current of the soul.

Full many a gem of purest ray serene,
   The dark unfathomed caves of ocean bear:

26. *glebe:* earth, soil.   51. *rage:* fire, enthusiasm, spirit, genius. (*Not* anger).

55   Full many a flower is born to blush unseen,
        And waste its sweetness on the desert air.

    Some village Hampden, that with dauntless breast
        The little Tyrant of his fields withstood;
    Some mute inglorious Milton here may rest,
60   Some Cromwell guiltless of his country's blood.

    The applause of listening senates to command,
        The threats of pain and ruin to despise,
    To scatter plenty o'er a smiling land,
        And read their history in a nation's eyes,

65   Their lot forbade: nor circumscribed alone
        Their growing virtues, but their crimes confined;
    Forbade to wade through slaughter to a throne,
        And shut the gates of mercy on mankind,

    The struggling pangs of conscious truth to hide,
70   To quench the blushes of ingenuous shame,
    Or heap the shrine of Luxury and Pride
        With incense kindled at the Muse's flame.

    Far from the madding crowd's ignoble strife,
        Their sober wishes never learned to stray;
75   Along the cool sequestered vale of life
        They kept the noiseless tenor of their way.

    Yet even these bones from insult to protect
        Some frail memorial still erected nigh,
    With uncouth rhymes and shapeless sculpture decked,
80   Implores the passing tribute of a sigh.

57. *Hampden:* John Hampden (1594-1643) famous as a leader of resistance to imposition of taxes by Charles I, killed in a skirmish at Chalgrove Field, near Oxford.

60. *Cromwell:* Oliver Cromwell (1599-1658) leader of the Parliamentary forces in the Civil War against Charles I, Lord Protector 1653-1658, mainly responsible for execution of the King.

76. *noiseless tenor:* quiet, accustomed, even way.

79. *uncouth:* unlearned, simple, ingenuous, naive.

Their name, their years, spelt by the unlettered Muse,
  The place of fame and elegy supply:
And many a holy text around she strews,
  That teach the rustic moralist to die.

For who to dumb Forgetfulness a prey,   85
  This pleasing anxious being e'er resigned,
Left the warm precincts of the cheerful day,
  Nor cast one longing lingering look behind?

On some fond breast the parting soul relies,
  Some pious drops the closing eye requires;   90
E'en from the tomb the voice of Nature cries,
  E'en in our Ashes live their wonted Fires.

For thee, who mindful of the unhonoured Dead
  Dost in these lines their artless tale relate,
If chance, by lonely contemplation led,   95
  Some kindred Spirit shall inquire thy fate,

Haply some hoary-headed Swain may say,
  "Oft have we seen him at the peep of dawn
Brushing with hasty steps the dews away
  To meet the sun upon the upland lawn.   100

"There at the foot of yonder nodding beech
  That wreathes its old fantastic roots so high,
His listless length at noontide would he stretch,
  And pore upon the brook that babbles by.

"Hard by yon wood, now smiling as in scorn,   105
  Muttering his wayward fancies he would rove,
Now drooping, woeful wan, like one forlorn,
  Or crazed with care, or crossed in hopeless love.

"One morn I missed him on the customed hill,
  Along the heath and near his favorite tree;   110
Another came; nor yet beside the rill,
  Nor up the lawn, nor at the wood was he;

97. *Swain:* country man.   105. *Hard by:* close by.

75

"The next with dirges due in sad array
　Slow through the church-way path we saw him borne.
Approach and read (for thou can'st read) the lay
　Graved on the stone beneath yon agéd thorn."

THE EPITAPH

Here rests his head upon the lap of earth
　A youth to fortune and to fame unknown.
Fair Science frowned not on his humble birth,
　And Melancholy marked him for her own.

Large was his bounty, and his soul sincere,
　Heaven did a recompense as largely send:
He gave to Misery all he had, a tear,
　He gained from Heaven ('twas all he wished) a friend.

No farther seek his merits to disclose,
　Or draw his frailties from their dread abode,
(There they alike in trembling hope repose)
　The bosom of his Father and his God.

WILLIAM COLLINS *1721-1759*

48 ⸱ *Ode to Evening*

If aught of oaten stop, or pastoral song,
May hope, chaste Eve, to soothe thy modest ear,
　Like thy own solemn springs,
　Thy springs and dying gales,

O nymph reserved, while now the bright-hair'd sun
Sits in yon western tent, whose cloudy skirts,
　With brede ethereal wove,
　O'erhang his wavy bed:

115. *read:* interpret, comprehend.　119. *Science:* study, learning.
　1. *oaten stop:* the stops of the pipe made of straw or reeds, symbolic of pastoral poetry.　7. *brede:* decorated border or edge.

Now air is hushed, save where the weak-eyed bat,
With short shrill shriek, flits by on leathern wing,   10
    Or where the beetle winds
    His small but sullen horn,

As oft he rises 'midst the twilight path,
Against the pilgrim borne in heedless hum.
    Now teach me, maid composed,   15
    To breathe some softened strain,

Whose numbers, stealing through thy dark'ning vale
May not unseemly with its stillness suit,
    As, musing slow, I hail
    Thy genial lov'd return!   20

For when thy folding-star arising shews
His paly circlet, at his warning lamp
    The fragrant Hours, the elves
    Who slept in flow'rs the day,

And many a nymph who wreaths her brows with sedge,   25
And sheds the fresh'ning dew, and, lovelier still
    The pensive Pleasures sweet,
    Prepare thy shadowy car.

Then lead, calm vot'ress, where some sheety lake
Cheers the lone heath, or some time-hallowed pile   30
    Or upland fallows grey
    Reflect its last cool gleam.

But when chill blust'ring winds, or driving rain,
Forbid my willing feet, be mine the hut
    That from the mountain's side   35
    Views wilds, and swelling floods,

And hamlets brown, and dim-discover'd spires,
And hears their simple bell, and marks o'er all

17. *numbers:* rhythms, harmonies.   20. *genial:* kindly.
21. *folding-star:* Evening star, that shines when sheep and cattle are brought in
to fold.

Thy dewy fingers draw
40   The gradual dusky veil.

While Spring shall pour his show'rs, as oft he wont,
And bathe thy breathing tresses, meekest Eve;
    While Summer loves to sport
    Beneath thy ling'ring light;

45 While sallow Autumn fills thy lap with leaves:
Or Winter, yelling through the troublous air,
    Affrights thy shrinking train,
    And rudely rends thy robes;

So long, sure-found beneath the sylvan shed,
50 Shall Fancy, Friendship, Science, rose-lipp'd Health,
    Thy gentlest influence own,
    And hymn thy fav'rite name!

WILLIAM BLAKE   *1757-1827*

49 *The Tyger*

Tyger! Tyger! burning bright
In the forests of the night,
What immortal hand or eye
Could frame thy fearful symmetry?

5   In what distant deeps or skies
Burnt the fire of thine eyes?
On what wings dare he aspire?
What the hand dare seize the fire?

And what shoulder, & what art,
10 Could twist the sinews of thy heart?
And when thy heart began to beat,
What dread hand? & what dread feet?

What the hammer? what the chain?
In what furnace was thy brain?
What the anvil? what dread grasp   15
Dare its deadly terrors clasp?

When the stars threw down their spears,
And water'd heaven with their tears,
Did he smile his work to see?
Did he who made the Lamb make thee?   20

Tyger! Tyger! burning bright
In the forests of the night,
What immortal hand or eye,
Dare frame thy fearful symmetry?

50 ⸗ Auguries of Innocence

To see a World in a Grain of Sand
And a Heaven in a Wild flower,
Hold Infinity in the palm of your hand,
And Eternity in an hour.

A Robin Redbreast in a Cage   5
Puts all Heaven in a Rage
A dove-house filled with Doves & Pigeons
Shudders Hell through all its regions.
A dog starved at his Master's Gate
Predicts the ruin of the State.   10
A Horse misused upon the Road
Calls to Heaven for Human blood.
Each outcry of the hunted Hare
A fibre from the Brain does tear.
A Skylark wounded in the wing,   15
A Cherubim does cease to sing;
The Game Cock clipped and armed for fight
Does the Rising Sun affright.
Every Wolf's & Lion's howl
Raises from Hell a Human Soul.   20

The wild Deer, wandering here & there,
Keeps the Human Soul from Care.
The Lamb misused breeds Public Strife
And yet forgives the Butcher's knife.
25 The Bat that flits at close of Eve
Has left the Brain that won't Believe.
The Owl that calls upon the Night
Speaks the Unbeliever's fright.
He who shall hurt the little Wren
30 Shall never be beloved by Men.
He who the Ox to wrath has moved
Shall never be by Woman loved.
The wanton Boy that kills the Fly
Shall fill the Spider's enmity.
35 He who torments the Chafer's Sprite
Weaves a Bower in endless Night.
The Caterpillar on the Leaf
Repeats to thee thy Mother's grief.
Kill not the Moth nor Butterfly,
40 For the Last Judgment draweth nigh.
He who shall train the Horse to war
Shall never pass the Polar Bar.
The Beggar's Dog & Widow's Cat,
Feed them & thou wilt grow fat.
45 The Gnat that sings his Summer's Song
Poison gets from Slander's tongue.
The poison of the Snake & Newt
Is the sweat of Envy's Foot.
The poison of the Honey Bee
50 Is the Artist's Jealousy.
The Prince's Robes & Beggar's Rags
Are Toadstools on the Miser's Bags.
A Truth that's told with bad intent
Beats all the Lies you can invent.
55 It is right it should be so;
Man was made for Joy & Woe;
And when this we rightly know,
Through the World we safely go.
Joy & Woe are woven fine,
60 A Clothing for the Soul divine.

80

Under every grief & pine
Runs a joy with silken twine.
The Babe is more than Swadling Bands;
Throughout all these Human Lands
Tools were made, & Born were hands,   65
Every Farmer understands.
Every Tear from Every Eye
Becomes a Babe in Eternity;
This is caught by Females bright,
And returned to its own delight.   70
The Bleat, the Bark, Bellow, & Roar
Are Waves that beat on Heaven's Shore.
The Babe that weeps the Rod beneath
Writes Revenge in realms of Death.
The Beggar's Rags, fluttering in Air,   75
Does to Rags the Heavens tear.
The Soldier, armed with Sword & Gun,
Palsied strikes the Summer's Sun.
The poor Man's Farthing is worth more
Than all the Gold on Afric's Shore.   80
One Mite wrung from the Lab'rer's hands
Shall buy & sell the Miser's Lands;
Or, if protected from on high,
Does that whole Nation sell & buy.
He who mocks the Infant's Faith   85
Shall be mocked in Age & Death.
He who shall teach the Child to Doubt
The rotting Grave shall ne'er get out.
He who respects the Infant's faith
Triumphs over Hell & Death.   90
The Child's Toys and the Old Man's Reasons
Are the Fruits of the Two Seasons.
The Questioner, who sits so sly,
Shall never know how to Reply.
He who replies to words of Doubt   95
Doth put the Light of Knowledge out.
The Strongest Poison ever known
Came from Caesar's Laurel Crown.
Naught can Deform the Human Race
Like to the Armour's iron brace.   100

When Gold and Gems adorn the Plow
To peaceful Arts shall Envy bow.
A Riddle, or the Cricket's Cry,
Is to Doubt a fit Reply.
105   The Emmet's Inch & Eagle's Mile
Make Lame Philosophy to smile.
He who Doubts from what he sees
Will ne'er Believe, do what you Please.
If the Sun & Moon should Doubt,
110   They'd immediately Go Out.
To be in a Passion you Good may do,
But no Good if a Passion is in you.
The Whore & Gambler, by the State
Licensed, build that Nation's Fate.
115   The Harlot's cry from Street to Street
Shall weave Old England's winding Sheet.
The Winner's shout, the Loser's Curse,
Dance before dead England's Hearse.
Every Night and every Morn
120   Some to Misery are Born.
Every Morn and every Night
Some are Born to Sweet Delight.
Some are Born to Sweet Delight,
Some are Born to Endless Night.
125   We are led to Believe a Lie
When we see not Through the Eye,
Which was Born in a Night to perish in a Night,
When the Soul slept in Beams of Light.
God appears, & God is light,
130   To those poor souls who dwell in Night,
But does a Human Form Display
To those who Dwell in Realms of Day.

51 ⸙ *London*

    I wander thro' each charter'd street,
    Near where the charter'd Thames does flow,

105. *Emmet*: ant.

82

And mark in every face I meet
Marks of weakness, marks of woe.

In every cry of every Man,   5
In every Infant's cry of fear,
In every voice, in every ban,
The mind-forg'd manacles I hear.

How the Chimney-sweeper's cry
Every black'ning Church appalls;   10
And the hapless Soldier's sigh
Runs in blood down Palace walls.

But most thro' midnight streets I hear
How the youthful Harlot's curse
Blasts the new born Infant's tear,   15
And blights with plagues the Marriage hearse.

ROBERT BURNS *1759-1796*

52 ▸ *To a Louse, on Seeing One on a Lady's
Bonnet at Church*

   Ha! where ye gaun, ye crowlan ferlie!
Your impudence protects you sairly:
I canna say but ye strunt rarely,
          Owre gawze and lace;
Tho' faith, I fear ye dine but sparely,   5
          On sic a place.

   Ye ugly, creepan, blastet wonner,
Detested, shunn'd, by saunt an' sinner,
How daur ye set your fit upon her,
          Sae fine a Lady!   10
Gae somewhere else and seek your dinner,
          On some poor body.

1. *ferlie*: wonder, marvel.   2. *sairly*: surely.   3. *strunt*: strut.
4. *gawze*: gauze.   6. *sic*: such.   7. *wonner*: wonder.

Swith, in some beggar's haffet squattle;
There ye may creep, and sprawl, and sprattle,
Wi' ither kindred, jumping cattle,
          In shoals and nations;
Whare horn nor bane ne'er daur unsettle
          Your thick plantations.

Now haud you there, ye're out o' sight,
Below the fatt'rels, snug and tight,
Na faith ye yet! ye'll no be right,
          Till ye've got on it,
The vera tapmost, towrin height
          O' Miss's bonnet.

My sooth! right bauld ye set your nose out,
As plump an' gray as onie grozet:
O for some rank, mercurial rozet,
          Or fell, red smeddum,
I'd gie you sic a hearty dose o't,
          Wad dress your droddum!

I wad na been surpriz'd to spy
You on an auld wife's flainen toy;
Or aiblins some bit duddie boy,
          On's wylecoat;
But Miss's fine Lunardi, fye!
          How daur ye do't?

O Jenny dinna toss your head,
An' set your beauties a' abread!
Ye little ken what cursed speed
          The blastie's makin!
Thae winks and finger-ends, I dread,
          Are notice takin!

O wad some Pow'r the giftie gie us
To see oursels as others see us!

---

13. *Swith:* quick.   *haffet:* temple.   19. *haud:* hold.
20. *fatt'rels:* ends of ribbons.   26. *grozet:* gooseberry.   27. *rozet:* rosin.
28. *smeddum:* powder.   30. *droddum:* breech.
32. *flainen toy:* flannel head-dress.   33. *aiblins:* perhaps.

It wad frae monie a blunder free us   45
    An' foolish notion:
What airs in dress an' gait wad lea'e us,
    And ev'n Devotion!

WILLIAM WORDSWORTH 1770-1850

53 ⸱ The Daffodils

I wandered lonely as a cloud
That floats on high o'er vales and hills,
When all at once I saw a crowd,
A host of golden daffodils;
Beside the lake, beneath the trees,   5
Fluttering and dancing in the breeze.

Continuous as the stars that shine
And twinkle on the milky way,
They stretched in never-ending line
Along the margin of a bay: 10
Ten thousand saw I at a glance,
Tossing their heads in sprightly dance.

The waves beside them danced; but they
Out-did the sparkling waves in glee.
A poet could not but be gay,   15
In such a jocund company:
I gazed—and gazed—but little thought
What wealth the show to me had brought:

For oft, when on my couch I lie
In vacant or in pensive mood,   20
They flash upon that inward eye
Which is the bliss of solitude;
And then my heart with pleasure fills,
And dances with the daffodils.

47. *wad led'e us:* would leave us.

Behold her, single in the field,
Yon solitary Highland Lass!
Reaping and singing by herself;
Stop here, or gently pass!
5   Alone she cuts and binds the grain,
And sings a melancholy strain;
O listen! for the Vale profound
Is overflowing with the sound.

No Nightingale did ever chant
10   More welcome notes to weary bands
Of travellers in some shady haunt,
Among Arabian sands:
A voice so thrilling ne'er was heard
In spring-time from the Cuckoo-bird,
15   Breaking the silence of the seas
Among the farthest Hebrides.

Will no one tell me what she sings?—
Perhaps the plaintive numbers flow
For old, unhappy, far-off things,
20   And battles long ago:
Or is it some more humble lay,
Familiar matter of to-day?
Some natural sorrow, loss, or pain,
That has been, and may be again?

25   Whate'er the theme, the maiden sang
As if her song could have no ending;
I saw her singing at her work,
And o'er the sickle bending;—
I listened, motionless and still;
30   And, as I mounted up the hill,
The music in my heart I bore
Long after it was heard no more.

Fair seed-time had my soul, and I grew up
Fostered alike by beauty and by fear:
Much favoured in my birthplace, and no less
In that beloved Vale to which erelong
We were transplanted—there were we let loose 5
For sports of wider range. Ere I had told
Ten birth-days, when among the mountain-slopes
Frost, and the breath of frosty wind, had snapped
The last autumnal crocus, 'twas my joy
With store of springes o'er my shoulder hung 10
To range the open heights where woodcocks run
Along the smooth green turf. Through half the night,
Scudding away from snare to snare, I plied
That anxious visitation;—moon and stars
Were shining o'er my head. I was alone, 15
And seemed to be a trouble to the peace
That dwelt among them. Sometimes it befell,
In these night wanderings, that a strong desire
O'erpowered my better reason, and the bird
Which was the captive of another's toil 20
Became my prey; and when the deed was done
I heard among the solitary hills
Low breathings coming after me, and sounds
Of undistinguishable motion, steps
Almost as silent as the turf they trod. 25

   Nor less when spring had warmed the cultured Vale,
Moved we as plunderers where the mother-bird
Had in high places built her lodge; though mean
Our object and inglorious, yet the end
Was not ignoble. Oh! when I have hung 30
Above the raven's nest, by knots of grass
And half-inch fissures in the slippery rock
But ill sustained, and almost (so it seemed)
Suspended by the blast that blew amain,
Shouldering the naked crag, oh! at that time 35
While on the perilous ridge I hung alone,
With what strange utterance did the loud dry wind

Blow through my ear! the sky seemed not a sky
Of earth—and with what motion moved the clouds!

40   Dust as we are, the immortal spirit grows
Like harmony in music; there is a dark
Inscrutable workmanship that reconciles
Discordant elements, and makes them cling together
In one society. How strange that all
45 The terrors, pains, and early miseries,
Regrets, vexations, lassitudes interfused
Within my mind, should e'er have borne a part,
And that a needful part, in making up
The calm existence that is mine when I
50 Am worthy of myself! Praise to the end!
Thanks to the means which Nature deigned to employ;
Whether her fearless visitings, or those
That came with soft alarm, like hurtless light
Opening the peaceful clouds; or she may use
55 Severer interventions, ministry
More palpable, as best might suit her aim.

    One summer evening (led by her) I found
A little boat tied to a willow tree
Within a rocky cove, its usual home.
60 Straight I unloosed her chain, and stepping in
Pushed from the shore. It was an act of stealth
And troubled pleasure, nor without the voice
Of mountain-echoes did my boat move on;
Leaving behind her still, on either side,
65 Small circles glittering idly in the moon,
Until they melted all into one track
Of sparkling light. But now, like one who rows,
Proud of his skill, to reach a chosen point
With an unswerving line, I fixed my view
70 Upon the summit of a craggy ridge,
The horizon's utmost boundary; far above
Was nothing but the stars and the gray sky.
She was an elfin pinnace; lustily
I dipped my oars into the silent lake,
75 And, as I rose upon the stroke, my boat

Went heaving through the water like a swan;
When, from behind that craggy steep, till then
The horizon's bound, a huge peak, black and huge,
As if with voluntary power instinct
Upreared its head. I struck and struck again,   80
And growing still in stature the grim shape
Towered up between me and the stars, and still,
For so it seemed, with purpose of its own
And measured motion like a living thing,
Strode after me. With trembling oars I turned,   85
And through the silent water stole my way
Back to the covert of the willow tree;
There in her mooring-place I left my bark,—
And through the meadows homeward went, in grave
And serious mood; but after I had seen   90
That spectacle, for many days, my brain
Worked with a dim and undetermined sense
Of unknown modes of being; o'er my thoughts
There hung a darkness, call it solitude
Or blank desertion. No familiar shapes   95
Remained, no pleasant images of trees,
Of sea or sky, no colours of green fields;
But huge and mighty forms, that do not live
Like living men, moved slowly through the mind
By day, and were a trouble to my dreams.   100

    Wisdom and Spirit of the universe!
Thou Soul that art the eternity of thought,
That givest to forms and images a breath
And everlasting motion, not in vain
By day or star-light thus from my first dawn   105
Of childhood didst thou intertwine for me
The passions that build up our human soul;
Not with the mean and vulgar works of man,
But with high objects, with enduring things—
With life and nature—purifying thus   110
The elements of feeling and of thought,
And sanctifying, by such discipline,
Both pain and fear, until we recognise
A grandeur in the beatings of the heart.

89

115 Nor was this fellowship vouchsafed to me
With stinted kindness. In November days,
When vapours rolling down the valley made
A lonely scene more lonesome, among woods,
At noon and 'mid the calm of summer nights,
120 When, by the margin of the trembling lake,
Beneath the gloomy hills homeward I went
In solitude, such intercourse was mine;
Mine was it in the fields both day and night,
And by the waters, all the summer long.

125   And in the frosty season, when the sun
Was set, and visible for many a mile
The cottage windows blazed through twilight gloom,
I heeded not their summons: happy time
It was indeed for all of us—for me
130 It was a time of rapture! Clear and loud
The village clock tolled six,—I wheeled about,
Proud and exulting like an untired horse
That cares not for his home. All shod with steel
We hissed along the polished ice in games
135 Confederate, imitative of the chase
And woodland pleasures,—the resounding horn,
The pack loud chiming, and the hunted hare.
So through the darkness and the cold we flew,
And not a voice was idle; with the din
140 Smitten, the precipices rang aloud;
The leafless trees and every icy crag
Tinkled like iron; while far distant hills
Into the tumult sent an alien sound
Of melancholy not unnoticed, while the stars
145 Eastward were sparkling clear, and in the west
The orange sky of evening died away.
Not seldom from the uproar I retired
Into a silent bay, or sportively
Glanced sideway, leaving the tumultuous throng,
150 To cut across the reflex of a star
That fled, and, flying still before me, gleamed
Upon the glassy plain; and oftentimes,
When we had given our bodies to the wind,

And all the shadowy banks on either side
Came sweeping through the darkness, spinning still   155
The rapid line of motion, then at once
Have I, reclining back upon my heels,
Stopped short; yet still the solitary cliffs
Wheeled by me—even as if the earth had rolled
With visible motion her diurnal round!   160
Behind me did they stretch in solemn train,
Feebler and feebler, and I stood and watched
Till all was tranquil as a dreamless sleep.

56 ⸱ *A Slumber Did My Spirit Seal*

A slumber did my spirit seal;
   I had no human fears:
She seem'd a thing that could not feel
   The touch of earthly years.

No motion has she now, no force;   5
   She neither hears nor sees;
Roll'd round in earth's diurnal course,
   With rocks, and stones, and trees.

57 ⸱ *The World Is Too Much with Us*

The world is too much with us; late and soon,
Getting and spending, we lay waste our powers:
Little we see in Nature that is ours;
We have given our hearts away, a sordid boon!
This Sea that bares her bosom to the moon;   5
The winds that will be howling at all hours,
And are up-gathered now like sleeping flowers;
For this, for everything, we are out of tune;
It moves us not.—Great God! I'd rather be
A Pagan suckled in a creed outworn;   10
So might I, standing on this pleasant lea,

Have glimpses that would make me less forlorn;
Have sight of Proteus rising from the sea;
Or hear old Triton blow his wreathéd horn.

SAMUEL TAYLOR COLERIDGE 1772-1834

58 ɪ Kubla Khan

In Xanadu did Kubla Khan
A stately pleasure-dome decree:
Where Alph, the sacred river, ran
Through caverns measureless to man
5   Down to a sunless sea.
     So twice five miles of fertile ground
      With walls and towers were girdled round:
And here were gardens bright with sinuous rills
Where blossomed many an incense-bearing tree;
10 And here were forests ancient as the hills,
Enfolding sunny spots of greenery.
But oh! that deep romantic chasm which slanted
Down the green hill athwart a cedarn cover!
A savage place! as holy and enchanted
15 As e'er beneath a waning moon was haunted
By woman wailing for her demon-lover!
And from this chasm, with ceaseless turmoil seething,
As if this earth in fast thick pants were breathing,
A mighty fountain momently was forced,
20 Amid whose swift half-intermitted burst
Huge fragments vaulted like rebounding hail,
Or chaffy grain beneath the thresher's flail:

13. *Proteus:* an old man of the sea, who tended the flocks of Poseidon. He had the gift of prophecy but he made it difficult for those who consulted him (such as Odysseus) by changing into many shapes and eluding their grasp.
14. *Triton:* a sea-god, son of Poseidon (Neptune).
  1. *Xanadu:* capital city of Kubla Khan (1214-94), Mongol emperor of China, the splendor of whose court was vividly described by Marco Polo.
  3. *Alph:* Coleridge's dream name formed from the sacred classical river Alpheus.

And 'mid these dancing rocks at once and ever
It flung up momently the sacred river.
Five miles meandering with a mazy motion   25
Through wood and dale the sacred river ran,
Then reached the caverns measureless to man,
And sank in tumult to a lifeless ocean:
And 'mid this tumult Kubla heard from far
Ancestral voices prophesying war!   30

    The shadow of the dome of pleasure
        Floated midway on the waves;
    Where was heard the mingled measure
        From the fountain and the caves.
It was a miracle of rare device,   35
A sunny pleasure-dome with caves of ice!

    A damsel with a dulcimer
    In a vision once I saw:
    It was an Abyssinian maid,
    And on her dulcimer she play'd,   40
    Singing of Mount Abora.
    Could I revive within me
    Her symphony and song,
To such a deep delight 'twould win me,
That with music loud and long,   45
I would build that dome in air,
That sunny dome! those caves of ice!
And all who heard should see them there,
And all should cry, Beware! Beware!
His flashing eyes, his floating hair!   50
Weave a circle round him thrice,
And close your eyes with holy dread,
For he on honey-dew hath fed,
And drunk the milk of Paradise.

30. *Ancestral voices:* Kubla was the grandson of the great conqueror Genghis
Khan.
37. *dulcimer:* strings stretched over a sounding board and struck with a hammer.
41. *Mount Abora:* Coleridge's dream name for a supposed mountain in Abyssinia.

59 ⊀ *So, We'll Go No More a-Roving*

So, we'll go no more a-roving
   So late into the night,
Though the heart be still as loving,
   And the moon be still as bright.

5   For the sword outwears its sheath,
   And the soul wears out the breast,
And the heart must pause to breathe,
   And love itself have rest.

Though the night was made for loving,
10   And the day returns too soon,
Yet we'll go no more a-roving
   By the light of the moon.

60 ⊀ *Ode to the West Wind*

I

O wild West Wind, thou breath of Autumn's being,
Thou, from whose unseen presence the leaves dead
Are driven, like ghosts from an enchanter fleeing,

Yellow, and black, and pale, and hectic red,
5   Pestilence-stricken multitudes: O thou,
Who chariotest to their dark wintry bed

The wingéd seeds, where they lie cold and low,
Each like a corpse within its grave, until
Thine azure sister of the spring shall blow

Her clarion o'er the dreaming earth, and fill   10
(Driving sweet buds like flocks to feed in air)
With living hues and odours plane and hill;

Wild Spirit, which art moving everywhere;
Destroyer and preserver; hear, Oh hear!

II

Thou on whose stream, 'mid the steep sky's commotion,   15
Loose clouds like earth's decaying leaves are shed,
Shook from the tangled boughs of Heaven and Ocean,

Angels of rain and lightning: there are spread
On the blue surface of thine airy surge,
Like the bright hair uplifted from the head   20

Of some fierce Mænad, even from the dim verge
Of the horizon to the zenith's height
The locks of the approaching storm. Thou dirge

Of the dying year, to which this closing night
Will be the dome of a vast sepulchre,   25
Vaulted with all thy congregated might

Of vapours, from whose solid atmosphere
Black rain, and fire, and hail will burst: Oh hear!

III

Thou who didst waken from his summer dreams
The blue Mediterranean, where he lay,   30
Lulled by the coil of his crystalline streams,

Beside a pumice isle in Baiæ's bay,
And saw in sleep old palaces and towers
Quivering within the wave's intenser day,

21. *Mænad:* a Bacchante, or priestess of Bacchus, the god of wine.
32. *Baiæ's bay:* the Bay of Naples. Baiae was a famous Roman pleasure resort, now covered by the sea.

35 All overgrown with azure moss and flowers
So sweet, the sense faints picturing them! Thou
For whose path the Atlantic's level powers

Cleave themselves into chasms, while far below
The sea-blooms and the oozy woods which wear
40 The sapless foliage of the ocean, know

Thy voice, and suddenly grow gray with fear,
And tremble and despoil themselves: Oh hear!

IV

If I were a dead leaf thou mightest bear;
If I were a swift cloud to fly with thee;
45 A wave to pant beneath thy power, and share

The impulse of thy strength, only less free
Than thou, O uncontrollable! If even
I were as in my boyhood, and could be

The comrade of thy wanderings over heaven,
50 As then, when to outstrip thy skiey speed
Scarce seemed a vision; I would ne'er have striven

As thus with thee in prayer in my sore need.
Oh! lift me as a wave, a leaf, a cloud!
I fall upon the thorns of life! I bleed!

55 A heavy weight of hours has chained and bowed
One too like thee: tameless, and swift, and proud.

V

Make me thy lyre, even as the forest is:
What if my leaves are falling like its own!
The tumult of thy mighty harmonies

60 Will take from both a deep, autumnal tone,
Sweet though in sadness. Be thou, spirit fierce,
My spirit! Be thou me, impetuous one!

Drive my dead thoughts over the universe
Like withered leaves to quicken a new birth!
And, by the incantation of this verse,   65

Scatter, as from an unextinguished hearth
Ashes and sparks, my words among mankind!
Be through my lips to unawakened earth

The trumpet of a prophecy! O, wind,
If Winter comes, can Spring be far behind?   70

61 ⸙ To a Skylark

Hail to thee, blithe spirit!
        Bird thou never wert—
    That from heaven or near it
        Pourest thy full heart
In profuse strains of unpremeditated art.   5

        Higher still and higher
            From the earth thou springest,
        Like a cloud of fire;
            The blue deep thou wingest,
And singing still dost soar, and soaring ever singest.   10

        In the golden light'ning
            Of the sunken sun,
        O'er which clouds are bright'ning,
            Thou dost float and run,
Like an unbodied joy whose race is just begun.   15

        The pale purple even
            Melts around thy flight;
        Like a star of heaven,
            In the broad daylight
Thou art unseen, but yet I hear thy shrill delight—   20

        Keen as are the arrows
            Of that silver sphere

97

Whose intense lamp narrows
        In the white dawn clear,
25 Until we hardly see, we feel that it is there.

        All the earth and air
        With thy voice is loud,
        As, when night is bare,
        From one lonely cloud
30 The moon rains out her beams, and heaven is overflow'd.

        What thou art we know not;
        What is most like thee?
        From rainbow clouds there flow not
        Drops so bright to see,
35 As from thy presence showers a rain of melody:—

        Like a poet hidden
        In the light of thought,
        Singing hymns unbidden,
        Till the world is wrought
40 To sympathy with hopes and fears it heeded not:

        Like a high-born maiden
        In a palace tower,
        Soothing her love-laden
        Soul in secret hour
45 With music sweet as love, which overflows her bower:

        Like a glow-worm golden
        In a dell of dew,
        Scattering unbeholden
        Its aërial hue
50 Among the flowers and grass which screen it from the view:

        Like a rose embower'd
        In its own green leaves,
        By warm winds deflower'd,
        Till the scent it gives
55 Makes faint with too much sweet those heavy-wingéd thieves.

Sound of vernal showers
On the twinkling grass,
Rain-awaken'd flowers—
All that ever was
Joyous and clear and fresh—thy music doth surpass.   60

Teach us, sprite or bird,
What sweet thoughts are thine:
I have never heard
Praise of love or wine
That panted forth a flood of rapture so divine.   65

Chorus hymeneal,
Or triumphal chant,
Match'd with thine would be all
But an empty vaunt—
A thing wherein we feel there is some hidden want.   70

What objects are the fountains
Of thy happy strain?
What fields, or waves, or mountains?
What shapes of sky or plain?
What love of thine own kind? what ignorance of pain?   75

With thy clear keen joyance
Languor cannot be:
Shadow of annoyance
Never came near thee:
Thou lovest, but ne'er knew love's sad satiety.   80

Waking or asleep,
Thou of death must deem
Things more true and deep
Than we mortals dream,
Or how could thy notes flow in such a crystal stream?   85

We look before and after,
And pine for what is not:

66. *Chorus hymeneal*: marriage hymn.

99

Our sincerest laughter
With some pain is fraught;
90 Our sweetest songs are those that tell of saddest thought.

Yet, if we could scorn
Hate and pride and fear,
If we were things born
Not to shed a tear,
95 I know not how thy joy we ever should come near.

Better than all measures
Of delightful sound,
Better than all treasures
That in books are found,
100 Thy skill to poet were, thou scorner of the ground!

Teach me half the gladness
That thy brain must know;
Such harmonious madness
From my lips would flow,
105 The world should listen then, as I am listening now.

62 *Ozymandias*

I met a traveller from an antique land
Who said: Two vast and trunkless legs of stone
Stand in the desert. Near them, on the sand,
Half sunk, a shattered visage lies, whose frown,
5 And wrinkled lip, and sneer of cold command,
Tell that its sculptor well those passions read
Which yet survive, stamped on these lifeless things,
The hand that mocked them and the heart that fed:
And on the pedestal these words appear:
10 "My name is Ozymandias, king of kings:
Look on my works, ye Mighty, and despair!"
Nothing beside remains. Round the decay
Of that colossal wreck, boundless and bare
The lone and level sands stretch far away.

63 1 *La Belle Dame Sans Merci*

"O what can ail thee, knight-at-arms,
　　Alone and palely loitering?
The sedge has wither'd from the lake,
　　And no birds sing.

"O what can ail thee, knight-at-arms,　　5
　　So haggard and so woe-begone?
The squirrel's granary is full,
　　And the harvest's done.

"I see a lily on thy brow
　　With anguish moist and fever dew;　　10
And on thy cheek a fading rose
　　Fast withereth too."

"I met a lady in the meads,
　　Full beautiful—a faery's child,
Her hair was long, her foot was light,　　15
　　And her eyes were wild.

"I made a garland for her head,
　　And bracelets too, and fragrant zone;
She look'd at me as she did love,
　　And made sweet moan.　　20

"I set her on my pacing steed
　　And nothing else saw all day long,
For side-ways would she lean, and sing
　　A faery's song.

"She found me roots of relish sweet,　　25
　　And honey wild, and manna dew,
And sure in language strange she said—
　　'I love thee true.'

"She took me to her elfin grot,
    And there she wept, and sigh'd full sore;
30 And there I shut her wild, wild eyes
        With kisses four.

"And there she lulléd me asleep,
    And there I dream'd—Ah! woe betide!
35 The latest dream I ever dream'd
        On the cold hill's side.

"I saw pale kings and princes too,
    Pale warriors, death-pale were they all;
Who cried—'La Belle Dame sans Merci
40   Hath thee in thrall!'

"I saw their starv'd lips in the gloom,
    With horrid warning gapéd wide,
And I awoke and found me here,
        On the cold hill's side.

45 "And this is why I sojourn here,
        Alone and palely loitering,
Though the sedge is wither'd from the lake,
        And no birds sing."

64 ⁊ Ode to a Nightingale

My heart aches, and a drowsy numbness pains
    My sense, as though of hemlock I had drunk,
Or emptied some dull opiate to the drains
    One minute past, and Lethe-wards had sunk:
5 'Tis not through envy of thy happy lot,
        But being too happy in thine happiness—
            That thou, light-winged Dryad of the trees,
                In some melodious plot

2. *hemlock*: poison used in the execution of Socrates.
4. *Lethe*: the river of Forgetfulness surrounding the Kingdom of the Dead in classical mythology.   7. *Dryad*: a spirit of the woods.

Of beechen green, and shadows numberless,
    Singest of summer in full-throated ease.   10

O, for a draught of vintage! that hath been
    Cool'd a long age in the deep-delved earth,
Tasting of Flora and the country green,
    Dance, and Provençal song, and sunburnt mirth!
O for a beaker full of the warm South,   15
    Full of the true, the blushful Hippocrene,
        With beaded bubbles winking at the brim,
            And purple-stained mouth;
    That I might drink, and leave the world unseen,
        And with thee fade away into the forest dim: 20

Fade far away, dissolve, and quite forget
    What thou among the leaves hast never known,
The weariness, the fever, and the fret
    Here, where men sit and hear each other groan;
Where palsy shakes a few, sad, last gray hairs,   25
    Where youth grows pale, and spectre-thin, and dies;
        Where but to think is to be full of sorrow
            And leaden-eyed despairs,
    Where Beauty cannot keep her lustrous eyes,
        Or new Love pine at them beyond to-morrow.   30

Away! away! for I will fly to thee,
    Not charioted by Bacchus and his pards,
But on the viewless wings of Poesy,
    Though the dull brain perplexes and retards:
Already with thee! tender is the night,   35
    And haply the Queen-Moon is on her throne,
        Cluster'd around by all her starry Fays;
            But here there is no light,
    Save what from heaven is with the breezes blown
        Through verdurous glooms and winding mossy ways.   40

13. *Flora:* the goddess of flowers and woods.
14. *Provençal song:* poetry and music like that of the medieval troubadours of Provence in the South of France.
16. *Hippocrene:* the richest and rarest of ancient Greek wines.
32. *Bacchus and his pards:* the god of wine riding in a car drawn by leopards.

I cannot see what flowers are at my feet,
    Nor what soft incense hangs upon the boughs,
But, in embalmed darkness, guess each sweet
    Wherewith the seasonable month endows
45 The grass, the thicket, and the fruit-tree wild;
    White hawthorn, and the pastoral eglantine;
      Fast fading violets cover'd up in leaves;
        And mid-May's eldest child,
    The coming musk-rose, full of dewy wine,
50   The murmurous haunt of flies on summer eves.

Darkling I listen; and, for many a time
    I have been half in love with easeful Death,
Call'd him soft names in many a mused rhyme,
    To take into the air my quiet breath;
55 Now more than ever seems it rich to die,
    To cease upon the midnight with no pain,
      While thou are pouring forth thy soul abroad
        In such an ecstasy!
    Still wouldst thou sing, and I have ears in vain—
60   To thy high requiem become a sod.

Thou wast not born for death, immortal Bird!
    No hungry generations tread thee down;
The voice I hear this passing night was heard
    In ancient days by emperor and clown:
65 Perhaps the self-same song that found a path
    Through the sad heart of Ruth, when, sick for home,
      She stood in tears amid the alien corn;
        The same that oft-times hath
    Charm'd magic casements, opening on the foam
70   Of perilous seas, in faery lands forlorn.

Forlorn! the very word is like a bell
    To toll me back from thee to my sole self!
Adieu! the fancy cannot cheat so well
    As she is fam'd to do, deceiving elf.

51. *Darkling*: in the dark.
66. *Ruth*: See the Book of Ruth in the Old Testament.

Adieu! adieu! thy plaintive anthem fades   75
    Past the near meadows, over the still stream,
        Up the hill-side; and now 'tis buried deep
            In the next valley-glades:
    Was it a vision, or a waking dream?
        Fled is that music:—Do I wake or sleep?   80

65 1 *Ode on a Grecian Urn*

Thou still unravish'd bride of quietness,
    Thou foster-child of silence and slow time,
Sylvan historian, who canst thus express
    A flowery tale more sweetly than our rhyme:
What leaf-fring'd legend haunts about thy shape   5
    Of deities or mortals, or of both,
        In Tempe or the dales of Arcady?
What men or gods are these? What maidens loth?
    What mad pursuit? What struggle to escape?
        What pipes and timbrels? What wild ecstasy?   10

Heard melodies are sweet, but those unheard
    Are sweeter; therefore, ye soft pipes, play on;
Not to the sensual ear, but, more endear'd,
    Pipe to the spirit ditties of no tone:
Fair youth, beneath the trees, thou canst not leave   15
    Thy song, nor ever can those trees be bare;
        Bold Lover, never, never canst thou kiss,
Though winning near the goal—yet, do not grieve;
    She cannot fade, though thou hast not thy bliss,
        For ever wilt thou love, and she be fair!   20

Ah, happy, happy boughs! that cannot shed
    Your leaves, nor ever bid the Spring adieu;
And, happy melodist, unwearied,
    For ever piping songs for ever new;
More happy love! more happy, happy love!   25
    For ever warm and still to be enjoy'd,
        For ever panting, and for ever young;
All breathing human passion far above,

105

That leaves a heart high-sorrowful and cloy'd,
30   A burning forehead, and a parching tongue.

Who are these coming to the sacrifice?
    To what green altar, O mysterious priest,
Lead'st thou that heifer lowing at the skies,
    And all her silken flanks with garlands dressed?
35 What little town by river or sea shore,
    Or mountain-built with peaceful citadel,
        Is emptied of this folk, this pious morn?
And, little town, thy streets for evermore
    Will silent be; and not a soul to tell
40   Why thou art desolate, can e'er return.

O Attic shape! Fair attitude! with brede
Of marble men and maidens overwrought
With forest branches and the trodden weed;
    Thou, silent form, dost tease us out of thought
45 As doth eternity: Cold Pastoral!
    When old age shall this generation waste,
        Thou shalt remain, in midst of other woe
Than ours, a friend to man, to whom thou say'st,
    "Beauty is truth, truth beauty,"—that is all
50   Ye know on earth, and all ye need to know.

66 ¹ To Autumn

Season of mists and mellow fruitfulness,
    Close bosom-friend of the maturing sun;
Conspiring with him how to load and bless
    With fruit the vines that round the thatch-eaves run;
5 To bend with apples the moss'd cottage-trees,
    And fill all fruit with ripeness to the core;
        To swell the gourd, and plump the hazel shells
With a sweet kernel; to set budding more,
    And still more, later flowers for the bees,
10   Until they think warm days will never cease,
        For Summer has o'er-brimmed their clammy cells.

Who hath not seen thee oft amid thy store?
　　Sometimes whoever seeks abroad may find
Thee sitting careless on a granary floor,
　　Thy hair soft-lifted by the winnowing wind;　　　15
Or on a half-reap'd furrow sound asleep,
　　Drows'd with the fume of poppies, while thy hook
　　　Spares the next swath and all its twined flowers:
And sometimes like a gleaner thou dost keep
　　Steady thy laden head across a brook;　　　20
　　Or by a cider-press, with patient look,
　　　Thou watchest the last oozings hours by hours.

Where are the songs of Spring? Ay, where are they?
　　Think not of them, thou hast thy music too,—
While barred clouds bloom the soft-dying day,　　　25
　　And touch the stubble-plains with rosy hue;
Then in a wailful choir the small gnats mourn
　　Among the river sallows, borne aloft
　　　Or sinking as the light wind lives or dies;
And full-grown lambs loud bleat from hilly bourn;　　　30
　　Hedge-crickets sing; and now with treble soft
　　The red-breast whistles from a garden-croft;
　　　And gathering swallows twitter in the skies.

67 ◦ Bright Star! Would I Were Steadfast as Thou Art

　　Bright star! would I were steadfast as thou art—
　　Not in lone splendor hung aloft the night,
　　And watching, with eternal lids apart,
　　Like Nature's patient sleepless Eremite,
　　The moving waters at their priestlike task　　　5
　　Of pure ablution round earth's human shores,
　　Or gazing on the new soft-fallen mask
　　Of snow upon the mountains and the moors—
　　No—yet still steadfast, still unchangeable,
　　Pillowed upon my fair love's ripening breast,　　　10
　　To feel for ever its soft fall and swell,
　　Awake for ever in a sweet unrest,

Still, still to hear her tender-taken breath,
And so live ever—or else swoon to death.

RALPH WALDO EMERSON   *1803-1882*

68 *1 Concord Hymn*
Sung at the Completion of the Battle Monument, July 4, 1837

By the rude bridge that arched the flood,
    Their flag to April's breeze unfurled,
Here once the embattled farmers stood
    And fired the shot heard round the world.

5   The foe long since in silence slept;
    Alike the conqueror silent sleeps;
And Time the ruined bridge has swept
    Down the dark stream which seaward creeps.

On this green bank, by this soft stream,
10   We set to-day a votive stone;
That memory may their deed redeem,
    When, like our sires, our sons are gone.

Spirit, that made those heroes dare
    To die, and leave their children free,
15   Bid Time and Nature gently spare
    The shaft we raise to them and thee.

HENRY WADSWORTH
LONGFELLOW   *1807-1882*

69 *1 My Lost Youth*

Often I think of the beautiful town
    That is seated by the sea;
Often in thought go up and down

1. *beautiful town*: Portland, Maine.

108

The pleasant streets of that dear old town,
  And my youth comes back to me.   5
    And a verse of a Lapland song
    Is haunting my memory still:
    "A boy's will is the wind's will,
And the thoughts of youth are long, long thoughts."

I can see the shadowy lines of its trees,   10
  And catch, in sudden gleams,
The sheen of the far-surrounding seas,
And islands that were the Hesperides
  Of all my boyish dreams.
    And the burden of that old song,   15
    It murmurs and whispers still:
    "A boy's will is the wind's will,
And the thoughts of youth are long, long thoughts."

I remember the black wharves and the slips,
  And the sea-tides tossing free;   20
And Spanish sailors with bearded lips,
And the beauty and mystery of the ships,
  And the magic of the sea.
    And the voice of that wayward song
    Is singing and saying still: 25
    "A boy's will is the wind's will,
And the thoughts of youth are long, long thoughts."

I remember the bulwarks by the shore,
  And the fort upon the hill;
The sunrise gun, with its hollow roar,   30
The drum-beat repeated o'er and o'er,
  And the bugle wild and shrill.
    And the music of that old song
    Throbs in my memory still:
    "A boy's will is the wind's will,   35
And the thoughts of youth are long, long thoughts."

I remember the sea-fight far away,
  How it thundered o'er the tide!
And the dead sea-captains, as they lay

40 In their graves, o'erlooking the tranquil bay
       Where they in battle died.
           And the sound of that mournful song
           Goes through me with a thrill:
           "A boy's will is the wind's will,
45 And the thoughts of youth are long, long thoughts."

   I can see the breezy dome of groves,
       The shadows of Deering's Woods;
   And the friendships old and the early loves
   Come back with a Sabbath sound, as of doves
50   In quiet neighborhoods.
           And the verse of that sweet old song,
           It flutters and murmurs still:
           "A boy's will is the wind's will,
   And the thoughts of youth are long, long thoughts."

55 I remember the gleams and glooms that dart
       Across the school-boy's brain;
   The song and the silence in the heart,
   That in part are prophecies, and in part
       Are longings wild and vain.
60   And the voice of that fitful song
           Sings on, and is never still:
           "A boy's will is the wind's will,
   And the thoughts of youth are long, long thoughts."

   There are things of which I may not speak;
65   There are dreams that cannot die;
   There are thoughts that make the strong heart weak,
   And bring a pallor into the cheek,
       And a mist before the eye.
           And the words of that fatal song
70   Come over me like a chill:
           "A boy's will is the wind's will,
   And the thoughts of youth are long, long thoughts."

   Strange to me now are the forms I meet
       When I visit the dear old town;
75 But the native air is pure and sweet,

110

And the trees that o'ershadow each well-known street,
  As they balance up and down,
    Are singing the beautiful song,
    Are sighing and whispering still:
    "A boy's will is the wind's will,   80
And the thoughts of youth are long, long thoughts."

And Deering's Woods are fresh and fair,
  And with joy that is almost pain
My heart goes back to wander there,
And among the dreams of the days that were,   85
  I find my lost youth again.
    And the strange and beautiful song,
    The groves are repeating it still:
    "A boy's will is the wind's will,
And the thoughts of youth are long, long thoughts."   90

EDGAR ALLAN POE *1809-1849*

70 ⚹ *To Helen*

    Helen, thy beauty is to me
      Like those Nicèan barks of yore
    That gently, o'er a perfumed sea,
      The weary way-worn wanderer bore
      To his own native shore.   5

    On desperate seas long wont to roam,
      Thy hyacinth hair, thy classic face,
    Thy Naiad airs have brought me home
      To the glory that was Greece,
    And the grandeur that was Rome.   10

    Lo, in yon brilliant window-niche
      How statue-like I see thee stand,
      The agate lamp within thy hand,
    Ah! Psyche, from the regions which
      Are holy land!   15

71 *1 The Lotos-Eaters*

"Courage!" he said, and pointed toward the land,
"This mounting wave will roll us shoreward soon."
In the afternoon they came unto a land
In which it seemed always afternoon.
5   All round the coast the languid air did swoon,
Breathing like one that hath a weary dream.
Full-faced above the valley stood the moon;
And like a downward smoke, the slender stream
Along the cliff to fall and pause and fall did seem.

10 A land of streams! some, like a downward smoke,
Slow-dropping veils of thinnest lawn, did go;
And some through wavering lights and shadows broke,
Rolling a slumbrous sheet of foam below.
They saw the gleaming river seaward flow
15 From the inner land: far off, three mountain-tops,
Three silent pinnacles of aged snow,
Stood sunset-flushed: and, dewed with showery drops,
Up-clomb the shadowy pine above the woven copse.

The charmed sunset lingered low adown
20 In the red West: through mountain clefts the dale
Was seen far inland, and the yellow down
Bordered with palm, and many a winding vale
And meadow, set with slender galingale;
A land where all things always seemed the same!
25 And round about the keel with faces pale,
Dark faces pale against that rosy flame,
The mild-eyed melancholy Lotos-eaters came.

Branches they bore of that enchanted stem,
Laden with flower and fruit, whereof they gave
30 To each, but whoso did receive of them,
And taste, to him the gushing of the wave

1. *he*: Odysseus. See Homer's *Odyssey*, Book IX.

Far far away did seem to mourn and rave
On alien shores; and if his fellow spake,
His voice was thin, as voices from the grave;
And deep-asleep he seemed, yet all awake,   35
And music in his ears his beating heart did make.

They sat them down upon the yellow sand,
Between the sun and moon upon the shore;
And sweet it was to dream of Fatherland,
Of child, and wife, and slave; but evermore   40
Most weary seemed the sea, weary the oar,
Weary the wandering fields of barren foam.
Then someone said, "We will return no more";
And all at once they sang, "Our island home
Is far beyond the wave; we will no longer roam."   45

CHORIC SONG

I

There is sweet music here that softer falls
Than petals from blown roses on the grass,
Or night-dews on still waters between walls
Of shadowy granite, in a gleaming pass;
Music that gentlier on the spirit lies,   50
Than tired eyelids upon tired eyes;
Music that brings sweet sleep down from the blissful skies.
Here are cool mosses deep,
And through the moss the ivies creep,
And in the stream the long-leaved flowers weep,   55
And from the craggy ledge the poppy hangs in sleep.

II

Why are we weighed upon with heaviness,
And utterly consumed with sharp distress,
While all things else have rest from weariness?
All things have rest: why should we toil alone,   60
We only toil, who are the first of things,
And make perpetual moan,

44. *Our island home:* Ithaca.

113

Still from one sorrow to another thrown:
Nor ever fold our wings,
65   And cease from wanderings,
Nor steep our brows in slumber's holy balm;
Nor hearken what the inner spirit sings,
    "There is no joy but calm!"—
Why should we only toil, the roof and crown of things?

III

70   Lo! in the middle of the wood,
The folded leaf is wooed from out the bud
With winds upon the branch, and there
Grows green and broad, and takes no care,
Sun-steeped at noon, and in the moon
75   Nightly dew-fed; and turning yellow
Falls, and floats adown the air.
Lo! sweetened with the summer light,
The full-juiced apple, waxing over-mellow,
Drops in a silent autumn night.
80   All its allotted length of days,
The flower ripens in its place,
Ripens and fades, and falls, and hath no toil,
Fast-rooted in the fruitful soil.

IV

Hateful is the dark-blue sky,
85   Vaulted o'er the dark-blue sea.
Death is the end of life; ah, why
Should life all labour be?
Let us alone. Time driveth onward fast,
And in a little while our lips are dumb.
90   Let us alone. What is it that will last?
All things are taken from us, and become
Portions and parcels of the dreadful past.
Let us alone. What pleasure can we have
To war with evil? Is there any peace
95   In ever climbing up the climbing wave?
All things have rest, and ripen toward the grave

In silence—ripen, fall and cease:
Give us long rest or death, dark death, or dreamful ease.

V

How sweet it were, hearing the downward stream,
With half-shut eyes ever to seem   100
Falling asleep in a half-dream!
To dream and dream, like yonder amber light,
Which will not leave the myrrh-bush on the height;
To hear each other's whispered speech;
Eating the Lotos day by day,   105
To watch the crisping ripples on the beach,
And tender curving lines of creamy spray;
To lend our hearts and spirits wholly
To the influence of mild-minded melancholy;
To muse and brood and live again in memory,   110
With those old faces of our infancy
Heaped over with a mound of grass,
Two handfuls of white dust, shut in an urn of brass!

VI

Dear is the memory of our wedded lives,
And dear the last embraces of our wives   115
And their warm tears: but all hath suffered change;
For surely now our household hearths are cold:
Our sons inherit us: our looks are strange:
And we should come like ghosts to trouble joy.
Or else the island princes over-bold   120
Have eat our substance, and the minstrel sings
Before them of the ten-years' war in Troy,
And our great deeds, as half-forgotten things.
Is there confusion in the little isle?
Let what is broken so remain.   125
The Gods are hard to reconcile:
'Tis hard to settle order once again.
There *is* confusion worse than death,
Trouble on trouble, pain on pain,
Long labour unto aged breath,   130

Sore task to hearts worn out with many wars
And eyes grown dim with gazing on the pilot-stars.

VII

But, propt on beds of amaranth and moly,
How sweet (while warm airs lull us, blowing lowly)
135 With half-dropt eyelids still,
Beneath a heaven dark and holy,
To watch the long bright river drawing slowly
His waters from the purple hill—
To hear the dewy echoes calling
140 From cave to cave through the thick-twined vine—
To watch the emerald-colored water falling
Through many a woven acanthus-wreath divine!
Only to hear and see the far-off sparkling brine,
Only to hear were sweet, stretched out beneath the pine.

VIII

145 The Lotos blooms below the barren peak:
The Lotos blows by every winding creek:
All day the wind breathes low with mellower tone:
Through every hollow cave and alley lone
Round and round the spicy downs the yellow Lotos-dust is
blown.
150 We have had enough of action, and of motion we,
Rolled to starboard, rolled to larboard, when the surge was
seething free,
Where the wallowing monster spouted his foam-fountains
in the sea.
Let us swear an oath, and keep it with an equal mind,
In the hollow Lotos-land to live and lie reclined
155 On the hills like Gods together, careless of mankind.
For they lie beside their nectar, and the bolts are hurled
Far below them in the valleys, and the clouds are lightly
curled
Round their golden houses, girdled with the gleaming
world:
Where they smile in secret, looking over wasted lands,
Blight and famine, plague and earthquake, roaring deeps
160   and fiery sands,

Clanging fights, and flaming towns, and sinking ships, and
    praying hands.
But they smile, they find a music centered in a doleful song
Steaming up, a lamentation and an ancient tale of wrong,
Like a tale of little meaning though the words are strong;
Chanted from an ill-used race of men that cleave the soil,   165
Sow the seed, and reap the harvest with enduring toil,
Storing yearly little dues of wheat, and wine and oil;
Till they perish and they suffer—some, 'tis whispered—
    down in hell
Suffer endless anguish, others in Elysian valleys dwell,
Resting weary limbs at last on beds of asphodel.   170
Surely, surely, slumber is more sweet than toil, the shore
Than labour in the deep mid-ocean, wind and wave and oar;
Oh, rest ye, brother mariners, we will not wander more.

72 ⁊ The Eagle

He clasps the crag with crooked hands;
Close to the sun in lonely lands,
Ring'd with the azure world he stands.

The wrinkled sea beneath him crawls;
He watches from his mountain walls,   5
And like a thunderbolt he falls.

73 ⁊ FROM In Memoriam: A.H.H.

XI

Calm is the morn without a sound,
    Calm as to suit a calmer grief,
    And only through the faded leaf
The chestnut pattering to the ground:

Calm and deep peace on this high wold,   5
    And on these dews that drench the furze,
    And all the silvery gossamers
That twinkle into green and gold:

A.H.H.: Arthur Henry Hallam, who died in Vienna, 1833.

Calm and still light on yon great plain
　　That sweeps with all its autumn bowers,
　　And crowded farms and lessening towers,
To mingle with the bounding main:

Calm and deep peace in this wide air,
　　These leaves that redden to the fall:
　　And in my heart, if calm at all,
If any calm, a calm despair:

Calm on the seas, and silver sleep,
　　And waves that sway themselves in rest,
　　And dead calm in that noble breast
Which heaves but with the heaving deep.

CI

Unwatch'd, the garden bough shall sway,
　　The tender blossom flutter down;
　　Unloved, that beech will gather brown,
This maple burn itself away;

Unloved, the sun-flower, shining fair,
　　Ray round with flames her disk of seed,
　　And many a rose-carnation feed
With summer spice the humming air;

Unloved, by many a sandy bar,
　　The brook shall babble down the plain,
　　At noon or when the lesser wain
Is twisting round the polar star;

Uncared for, gird the windy grove,
　　And flood the haunts of hern and crake;
　　Or into silver arrows break
The sailing moon in creek and cove;

17. *Calm on the seas:* This stanza refers to the calm seas through which the ship bearing the body of Arthur Hallam home for burial is sailing as the poet meditates in England.

Till from the garden and the wild
   A fresh association blow,
   And year by year the landscape grow
Familiar to the stranger's child;   20

As year by year the labourer tills
   His wonted glebe, or lops the glades;
   And year by year our memory fades
From all the circle of the hills.

ROBERT BROWNING *1812-1889*

74 ⁊ *My Last Duchess*
FERRARA

That's my last Duchess painted on the wall,
Looking as if she were alive. I call
That piece a wonder, now: Frà Pandolf's hands
Worked busily a day, and there she stands.
Will't please you sit and look at her? I said   5
"Frà Pandolf" by design, for never read
Strangers like you that pictured countenance,
The depth and passion of its earnest glance,
But to myself they turned (since none puts by
The curtain I have drawn for you, but I)   10
And seemed as they would ask me, if they durst,
How such a glance came there; so, not the first
Are you to turn and ask thus. Sir, 'twas not
Her husband's presence only, called that spot
Of joy into the Duchess' cheek; perhaps   15
Frà Pandolf chanced to say, "Her mantle laps
Over my lady's wrist too much," or "Paint
Must never hope to reproduce the faint
Half-flush that dies along her throat": such stuff
Was courtesy, she thought, and cause enough   20
For calling up that spot of joy. She had
A heart—how shall I say?—too soon made glad,
Too easily impressed: she liked whate'er

She looked on, and her looks went everywhere.
25 Sir, 'twas all one! My favour at her breast,
The dropping of the daylight in the West,
The bough of cherries some officious fool
Broke in the orchard for her, the white mule
She rode with round the terrace—all and each
30 Would draw from her alike the approving speech,
Or blush, at least. She thanked men,—good! but thanked
Somehow—I know not how—as if she ranked
My gift of a nine-hundred-years-old name
With anybody's gift. Who'd stoop to blame
35 This sort of trifling? Even had you skill
In speech—(which I have not)—to make your will
Quite clear to such an one, and say, "Just this
Or that in you disgusts me; here you miss,
Or there exceed the mark"—and if she let
40 Herself be lessoned so, nor plainly set
Her wits to yours, forsooth, and made excuse,
—E'en then would be some stooping; and I choose
Never to stoop. Oh sir, she smiled, no doubt,
Whene'er I passed her; but who passed without
45 Much the same smile? This grew; I gave commands;
Then all smiles stopped together. There she stands
As if alive. Will't please you rise? We'll meet
The company below, then. I repeat,
The Count your master's known munificence
50 Is ample warrant that no just pretence
Of mine for dowry will be disallowed;
Though his fair daughter's self, as I avowed
At starting, is my object. Nay, we'll go
Together down, sir. Notice Neptune, though,
55 Taming a sea-horse, thought a rarity,
Which Claus of Innsbruck cast in bronze for me!

75 ◆ The Bishop Orders His Tomb at Saint Praxed's Church

Vanity, saith the preacher, vanity!
Draw round my bed: is Anselm keeping back?
Nephews—sons mine . . . ah God, I know not! Well—
She, men would have to be your mother once,
Old Gandolf envied me, so fair she was!   5
What's done is done, and she is dead beside,
Dead long ago, and I am Bishop since,
And as she died so must we die ourselves,
And thence ye may perceive the world's a dream.
Life, how and what is it? As here I lie   10
In this state-chamber, dying by degrees,
Hours and long hours in the dead night, I ask,
"Do I live, am I dead?" Peace, peace seems all.
Saint Praxed's ever was the church for peace;
And so, about this tomb of mine. I fought   15
With tooth and nail to save my niche, ye know:
—Old Gandolf cozened me, despite my care;
Shrewd was that snatch from out the corner South
He graced his carrion with, God curse the same!
Yet still my niche is not so cramped but thence   20
One sees the pulpit o' the epistle-side,
And somewhat of the choir, those silent seats,
And up into the aery dome where live
The angels, and a sunbeam's sure to lurk:
And I shall fill my slab of basalt there,   25
And 'neath my tabernacle take my rest,
With those nine columns round me, two and two,
The odd one at my feet where Anselm stands:
Peach-blossom marble all, the rare, the ripe
As fresh-poured red wine of a mighty pulse.   30
—Old Gandolf with his paltry onion-stone,

St. Praxed's Church: in Rome. A real church, though the characters and story are imaginary.

1. *Vanity, saith the preacher:* Ecclesiastes I:2.
5. *Old Gandolf:* his predecessor and rival.

121

Put me where I may look at him! True peach,
Rosy and flawless: how I earned the prize!
Draw close: that conflagration of my church
35 —What then? So much was saved if aught were missed!
My sons, ye would not be my death? Go dig
The white-grape vineyard where the oil-press stood,
Drop water gently till the surface sink,
And if ye find . . . ah God, I know not, I! . . .
40 Bedded in store of rotten fig-leaves soft,
And corded up in a tight olive-frail,
Some lump, ah God, of *lapis lazuli,*
Big as a Jew's head cut off at the nape,
Blue as a vein o'er the Madonna's breast . . .
45 Sons, all have I bequeathed you, villas, all,
That brave Frascati villa with its bath,
So, let the blue lump poise between my knees,
Like God the Father's globe on both his hands
Ye worship in the Jesu Church so gay,
50 For Gandolf shall not choose but see and burst!
Swift as a weaver's shuttle fleet our years:
Man goeth to the grave, and where is he?
Did I say basalt for my slab, sons? Black—
'Twas ever antique-black I meant! How else
55 Shall ye contrast my frieze to come beneath?
The bas-relief in bronze ye promised me,
Those Pans and Nymphs ye wot of, and perchance
Some tripod, thyrsus, with a vase or so,
The Savior at his sermon on the mount,
60 Saint Praxed in a glory, and one Pan
Ready to twitch the Nymph's last garment off,
And Moses with the tables . . . but I know
Ye mark me not! What do they whisper thee,
Child of my bowels, Anselm? Ah, ye hope
65 To revel down my villas while I gasp
Bricked o'er with beggar's moldy travertine
Which Gandolf from his tomb-top chuckles at!
Nay, boys, ye love me—all of jasper, then!
'Tis jasper ye stand pledged to, lest I grieve.

41. *olive-frail:* olive basket.

My bath must needs be left behind, alas!   70
One block, pure green as a pistachio-nut,
There's plenty jasper somewhere in the world—
And have I not Saint Praxed's ear to pray
Horses for ye, and brown Greek manuscripts,
And mistresses with great smooth marbly limbs?   75
—That's if ye carve my epitaph aright,
Choice Latin, picked phrase, Tully's every word,
No gaudy ware like Gandolf's second line—
Tully, my masters! Ulpian serves his need!
And then how I shall lie through centuries,   80
And hear the blessed mutter of the mass,
And see God made and eaten all day long,
And feel the steady candle-flame, and taste
Good, strong, thick, stupefying incense-smoke!
For as I lie here, hours of the dead night,   85
Dying in state and by such slow degrees,
I fold my arms as if they clasped a crook,
And stretch my feet forth straight as stone can point,
And let the bedclothes, for a mortcloth, drop
Into great laps and folds of sculptor's-work: 90
And as yon tapers dwindle, and strange thoughts
Grow, with a certain humming in my ears,
About the life before I lived this life,
And this life too, popes, cardinals and priests,
Saint Praxed at his sermon on the mount,   95
Your tall pale mother with her talking eyes,
And new-found agate urns as fresh as day,
And marble's language, Latin pure, discreet,
—Aha, ELUCESCEBAT quoth our friend?
No Tully, said I, Ulpian at the best!   100
Evil and brief hath been my pilgrimage.
All *lapis,* all, sons! Else I give the Pope
My villas! Will ye ever eat my heart?
Ever your eyes were as a lizard's quick,
They glitter like your mother's for my soul,   105
Or ye would heighten my impoverished frieze,

79. *Ulpian:* Roman jurist with a debased style.
99. ELUCESCEBAT: He was famous. Not in the pure Latin of Cicero (Tully) but in the debased style of Ulpian.

Piece out its starved design, and fill my vase
With grapes, and add a visor and a Term,
And to the tripod ye would tie a lynx
110   That in his struggle throws the thyrsus down,
To comfort me on my entablature
Whereon I am to lie till I must ask,
"Do I live, am I dead?" There, leave me, there!
For ye have stabbed me with ingratitude
115   To death—ye wish it—God, ye wish it! Stone—
Gritstone, a-crumble! Clammy squares which sweat
As if the corpse they keep were oozing through—
And no more *lapis* to delight the world!
Well, go! I bless ye. Fewer tapers there,
120   But in a row: and, going, turn your backs
—Aye, like departing altar-ministrants,
And leave me in my church, the church for peace,
That I may watch at leisure if he leers—
Old Gandolf—at me, from his onion-stone,
125   As still he envied me, so fair she was!

WALT WHITMAN   *1819-1892*

76 *1 Out of the Cradle Endlessly Rocking*

Out of the cradle endlessly rocking,
Out of the mocking-bird's throat, the musical shuttle,
Out of the Ninth-month midnight,
Over the sterile sands, and the fields beyond, where the child,
     leaving his bed, wander'd alone, bareheaded, barefoot,
5   Down from the shower'd halo,
Up from the mystic play of shadows, twining and twisting as
     if they were alive,
Out from the patches of briers and blackberries,
From the memories of the bird that chanted to me,
From your memories, sad brother—from the fitful risings and
     fallings I heard,
10   From under that yellow half-moon, late-risen, and swollen as
     if with tears,

From those beginning notes of sickness and love, there in the
    transparent mist,
From the thousand responses of my heart, never to cease,
From the myriad thence-aroused words,
From the word stronger and more delicious than any,
From such, as now they start, the scene revisiting,   15
As a flock, twittering, rising, or overhead passing,
Borne hither—ere all eludes me, hurriedly,
A man—yet by these tears a little boy again,
Throwing myself on the sand, confronting the waves,
I, chanter of pains and joys, uniter of here and hereafter,   20
Taking all hints to use them—but swiftly leaping beyond
    them,
A reminiscence sing.

Once, Paumanok,
When the snows had melted—when the lilac-scent was in the
    air, and the Fifth-month grass was growing,
Up this sea-shore, in some briers,   25
Two guests from Alabama—two together,
And their nest, and four light-green eggs, spotted with brown,
And every day the he-bird, to and fro, near at hand,
And every day the she-bird, crouch'd on her nest, silent, with
    bright eyes,
And every day I, a curious boy, never too close, never
    disturbing them,
Cautiously peering, absorbing, translating.   30

Shine! shine! shine!
Pour down your warmth, great Sun!
While we bask—we two together.

Two together!   35
Winds blow South, or winds blow North,
Day come white, or night come black,
Home, or rivers and mountains from home,
Singing all time, minding no time,
While we two keep together.   40

Till of a sudden,
May-be kill'd, unknown to her mate,
One forenoon the she-bird crouch'd not on the nest,
Nor return'd that afternoon, nor the next,
45 Nor ever appear'd again.
And thenceforward, all summer, in the sound of the sea,
And at night, under the full of the moon, in calmer weather,
Over the hoarse surging of the sea,
Or flitting from brier to brier by day,
50 I saw, I heard at intervals, the remaining one, the he-bird,
The solitary guest from Alabama.

Blow! blow! blow!
Blow up, sea-winds, along Paumanok's shore!
I wait and I wait, till you blow my mate to me.

55 Yes, when the stars glisten'd,
All night long, on the prong of a moss-scallop'd stake,
Down, almost amid the slapping waves,
Sat the lone singer, wonderful, causing tears.

He call'd on his mate;
60 He pour'd forth the meanings which I, of all men, know.

Yes, my brother, I know;
The rest might not—but I have treasured every note;
For once, and more than once, dimly, down to the beach
    gliding,
Silent, avoiding the moonbeams, blending myself with the
    shadows,
65 Recalling now the obscure shapes, the echoes, the sounds and
    sights after their sorts,
The white arms out in the breakers tirelessly tossing,
I, with bare feet, a child, the wind wafting my hair,
Listen'd long and long.

Listen'd, to keep, to sing—now translating the notes,
70 Following you, my brother.

Soothe! soothe! soothe!
Close on its wave soothes the wave behind,
And again another behind, embracing and lapping, every one
    close,
But my love soothes not me, not me.

Low hangs the moon—it rose late;   75
O it is lagging—O I think it is heavy with love, with love.

O madly the sea pushes, pushes upon the land,
With love—with love.

O night! do I not see my love fluttering out there among the
    breakers?
What is that little black thing I see there in the white?   80

Loud! loud! loud!
Loud I call to you, my love!
High and clear I shoot my voice over the waves;
Surely you must know who is here, is here;
You must know who I am, my love.   85

Low-hanging moon!
What is that dusky spot in your brown yellow?
O it is the shape, the shape of my mate!
O moon, do not keep her from me any longer.

Land! land! O land!   90
Whichever way I turn, O I think you could give me my mate
    back again, if you only would;
For I am almost sure I see her dimly whichever way I look.

O rising stars!
Perhaps the one I want so much will rise, will rise with some
    of you.

O throat! O trembling throat!   95
Sound clearer through the atmosphere!
Pierce the woods, the earth;
Somewhere listening to catch you, must be the one I want.

Shake out, carols!
100 Solitary here—the night's carols!
Carols of lonesome love! Death's carols!
Carols under that lagging, yellow, waning moon!
O, under that moon, where she droops almost down into the
sea!
O reckless, despairing carols.

105 But soft! sink low;
Soft! let me just murmur;
And do you wait a moment, you husky-noised sea;
For somewhere I believe I heard my mate responding to me,
So faint—I must be still, be still to listen;
But not altogether still, for then she might not come
110 immediately to me.

Hither, my love!
Here I am! Here!
With this just-sustain'd note I announce myself to you;
This gentle call is for you, my love, for you.

115 Do not be decoy'd elsewhere!
That is the whistle of the wind—it is not my voice;
That is the fluttering, the fluttering of the spray;
Those are the shadows of leaves.

O darkness! O in vain!
120 O I am very sick and sorrowful.

O brown halo in the sky, near the moon, drooping upon the
sea!
O troubled reflection in the sea!
O throat! O throbbing heart!
O all—and I singing uselessly, uselessly all the night.

125 Yet I murmur, murmur on!
O murmurs—you yourselves make me continue to sing, I
know not why.

O past! O life! O songs of joy!
In the air—in the woods—over fields;
Loved! loved! loved! loved! loved!
But my love no more, no more with me!   130
We two together no more.

The aria sinking;
All else continuing—the stars shining,
The winds blowing—the notes of the bird continuous echoing,
With angry moans the fierce old mother incessantly moaning,   135
On the sands of Paumanok's shore, grey and rustling;
The yellow half-moon enlarged, sagging down, drooping, the
    face of the sea almost touching;
The boy ecstatic—with his bare feet the waves, with his hair
    the atmosphere dallying,
The love in the heart long pent, now loose, now at last
    tumultuously bursting,
The aria's meaning, the ears, the Soul, swiftly depositing,   140
The strange tears down the cheeks coursing,
The colloquy there—the trio—each uttering,
The undertone—the savage old mother, incessantly crying,
To the boy's Soul's questions sullenly timing—some drown'd
    secret hissing,
To the outsetting bard of love.   145

Demon or bird! (said the boy's soul,)
Is it indeed toward your mate you sing? or is it mostly to me?
For I, that was a child, my tongue's use sleeping,
Now I have heard you,
Now in a moment I know what I am for—I awake,   150
And already a thousand singers—a thousand songs, clearer,
    louder and more sorrowful than yours,
A thousand warbling echoes have started to life within me,
Never to die.

O you singer, solitary, singing by yourself—projecting me;
O solitary me, listening—never more shall I cease perpetuating
    you;   155
Never more shall I escape, never more the reverberations,
Never more the cries of unsatisfied love be absent from me,

129

Never again leave me to be the peaceful child I was before
     what there, in the night,
By the sea, under the yellow and sagging moon,
160 The messenger there aroused—the fire, the sweet hell within,
The unknown want, the destiny of me.
O give me the clue! (it lurks in the night here somewhere;)
O if I am to have so much, let me have more!
O a word! O what is my destination? (I fear it is henceforth
     chaos;)
O how joys, dreads, convolutions, human shapes, and all
165   shapes, spring as from graves around me!
O phantoms! you cover all the land and all the sea!
O I cannot see in the dimness whether you smile or frown
     upon me;
O vapour, a look, a word! O well-beloved!
O you dear women's and men's phantoms!
170 A word then, (for I will conquer it,)
The word final, superior to all,
Subtle, sent up—what is it?—I listen;
Are you whispering it, and have been all the time, you sea-
     waves?
Is that it from your liquid rims and wet sands?

175 Whereto answering, the sea,
Delaying not, hurrying not,
Whisper'd me through the night, and very plainly before
     daybreak,
Lisp'd to me the low and delicious word Death;
And again Death—ever Death, Death, Death,
Hissing melodious, neither like the bird, nor like my aroused
180   child's heart,
But edging near, as privately for me, rustling at my feet,
Creeping thence steadily up to my ears, and laving me softly
     all over,
Death, Death, Death, Death, Death.

Which I do not forget,
185 But fuse the song of my dusky demon and brother,
That he sang to me in the moonlight on Paumanok's grey
     beach,

With the thousand responsive songs, at random,
My own songs, awaked from that hour;
And with them the key, the word up from the waves,
The word of the sweetest song, and all songs,   190
That strong and delicious word which, creeping to my feet,
The sea whisper'd me.

MATTHEW ARNOLD *1822-1888*

77 ⸸ *Dover Beach*

    The sea is calm to-night.
    The tide is full, the moon lies fair
    Upon the straits;—on the French coast the light
    Gleams and is gone; the cliffs of England stand,
    Glimmering and vast, out in the tranquil bay.   5
    Come to the window, sweet is the night air!
    Only, from the long line of spray
    Where the sea meets the moon-blanched land,
    Listen! you hear the grating roar
    Of pebbles which the waves draw back, and fling,   10
    At their return, up the high strand,
    Begin, and cease, and then again begin,
    With tremulous cadence slow, and bring
    The eternal note of sadness in.

    Sophocles long ago   15
    Heard it on the Ægean, and it brought
    Into his mind the turbid ebb and flow
    Of human misery; we
    Find also in the sound a thought,
    Hearing it by this distant northern sea   20

    The Sea of Faith
    Was once, too, at the full, and round earth's shore
    Lay like the folds of a bright girdle furled.
    But now I only hear
    Its melancholy, long, withdrawing roar,   25

Retreating, to the breath
Of the night wind, down the vast edges drear
And naked shingles of the world.

Ah, love, let us be true
30 To one another! for the world, which seems
To lie before us like a land of dreams,
So various, so beautiful, so new,
Hath really neither joy, nor love, nor light,
Nor certitude, nor peace, nor help for pain;
35 And we are here as on a darkling plain
Swept with confused alarms of struggle and flight
Where ignorant armies clash by night.

DANTE GABRIEL ROSSETTI *1828-1882*

78 ⚊ *The Blessed Damozel*

The blessed Damozel leaned out
    From the gold bar of Heaven;
Her eyes were deeper than the depth
    Of waters stilled at even;
5 She had three lilies in her hand,
    And the stars in her hair were seven.

Her robe, ungirt from clasp to hem,
    No wrought flowers did adorn,
But a white rose of Mary's gift,
10   For service meetly worn;
Her hair that lay along her back
    Was yellow like ripe corn.

Herseemed she scarce had been a day
    One of God's choristers;
15 The wonder was not yet quite gone
    From that still look of hers;
Albeit, to them she left, her day
    Had counted as ten years.

(To one it is ten years of years:
   . . . Yet now, here in this place,
Surely she leaned o'er me,—her hair
   Fell all about my face. . . .
Nothing: the autumn fall of leaves.
   The whole year sets apace.)

It was the rampart of God's house
   That she was standing on;
By God built over the sheer depth
   In which is Space begun;
So high, that looking downward thence,
   She scarce could see the sun.

It lies in Heaven, across the flood
   Of ether, as a bridge.
Beneath, the tides of day and night
   With flame and darkness ridge
The void, as low as where this earth
   Spins like a fretful midge.

Around her, lovers, newly met
   'Mid deathless love's acclaims,
Spoke evermore among themselves
   Their heart-remembered names;
And the souls, mounting up to God,
   Went by her like thin flames.

And still she bowed herself, and stooped
   Out of the circling charm;
Until her bosom must have made
   The bar she leaned on warm,
And the lilies lay as if asleep
   Along her bended arm.

From the fixed place of Heaven, she saw
   Time, like a pulse, shake fierce
Through all the worlds. Her gaze still strove
   Within the gulf to pierce
Its path; and now she spoke as when
   The stars sang in their spheres.

The sun was gone now; the curled moon
    Was like a little feather
Fluttering far down the gulf; and now
    She spoke through the still weather.
Her voice was like the voice the stars
    Had when they sang together.

(Ah sweet! Even now, in that bird's song,
    Strove not her accents there,
Fain to be hearkened? When those bells
    Possessed the mid-day air,
Strove not her steps to reach my side
    Down all the echoing stair?)

"I wish that he were come to me,
    For he will come," she said.
"Have I not prayed in Heaven? on earth
    Lord, Lord, has he not prayed?
Are not two prayers a perfect strength?
    And shall I feel afraid?

"When round his head the aureole clings,
    And he is clothed in white,
I'll take his hand and go with him
    To the deep wells of light;
We will step down as to a stream,
    And bathe there in God's sight.

"We two will stand beside that shrine,
    Occult, withheld, untrod,
Whose lamps are stirred continually
    With prayer sent up to God;
And see our old prayers granted, melt
    Each like a little cloud.

"We two will lie i' the shadow of
    That living mystic tree
Within whose secret growth the Dove
    Is sometimes felt to be,

While every leaf that His plumes touch
　　Saith His Name audibly. 90

"And I myself will teach to him,
　　I myself, lying so,
The songs I sing here; which his voice
　　Shall pause in, hushed and slow,
And find some knowledge at each pause, 95
　　Or some new thing to know."

(Alas! we two, we two, thou say'st!
　　Yea, one wast thou with me
That once of old. But shall God lift
　　To endless unity 100
The soul whose likeness with thy soul
　　Was but its love for thee?)

"We two," she said, "will seek the groves
　　Where the lady Mary is,
With her five handmaidens, whose names 105
　　Are five sweet symphonies:—
Cecily, Gertrude, Magdalen,
　　Margaret and Rosalys.

"Circlewise sit they, with bound locks
　　And foreheads garlanded; 110
Into the fine cloth white like flame,
　　Weaving the golden thread,
To fashion the birth-robes for them
　　Who are just born, being dead.

"He shall fear, haply, and be dumb: 115
　　Then will I lay my cheek
To his, and tell about our love,
　　Not once abashed or weak:
And the dear Mother will approve
　　My pride, and let me speak. 120

"Herself shall bring us, hand in hand,
　　To Him round whom all souls

Kneel, the clear-ranged unnumbered heads
    Bowed with their aureoles:
And angels, meeting us, shall sing
    To their citherns and citoles.

"There will I ask of Christ the Lord
    Thus much for him and me:—
Only to live as once on earth
    With Love,—only to be,
As then awhile, for ever now
    Together, I and he."

She gazed, and listened, and then said,
    Less sad of speech than mild,—
"All this is when he comes." She ceased.
    The light thrilled towards her, filled
With angels, in strong level flight.
    Her eyes prayed, and she smiled.

(I saw her smile.) But soon their path
    Was vague in distant spheres.
And then she cast her arms along
    The golden barriers,
And laid her face between her hands,
    And wept. (I heard her tears.)

EMILY DICKINSON *1830-1886*

79 ɪ *Because I Could Not Stop for Death*

Because I could not stop for Death—
He kindly stopped for me—
The Carriage held but just Ourselves—
And Immortality.

We slowly drove—He knew no haste
And I had put away

136

My labor and my leisure too,
For His Civility—

We passed the School, where Children strove
At Recess—in the Ring—   10
We passed the Fields of Gazing Grain—
We passed the Setting Sun—

Or rather—He passed Us—
The Dews drew quivering and chill—
For only Gossamer, my Gown—   15
My Tippet—only Tulle—

We paused before a House that seemed
A Swelling of the Ground—
The Roof was scarcely visible—
The Cornice—in the Ground—   20

Since then—'tis Centuries—and yet
Feels shorter than the Day
I first surmised the Horses Heads
Were toward Eternity—

ALGERNON CHARLES
SWINBURNE *1837-1909*

80 ✶ *The Garden of Proserpine*

Here, where the world is quiet;
    Here, where all trouble seems
Dead winds' and spent waves' riot

Proserpine: The Garden of Proserpine: Proserpine (Persephone) was the daughter of Jupiter (Zeus) and Ceres (Demeter), the Earth-Mother. She was carried off by Pluto, while gathering flowers in the fields of Enna in Sicily, and made Queen of Hades, the kingdom of the dead. At the instigation of Jupiter, Proserpine was allowed to return to the earth in spring and to spend half of the year with her mother and half with Pluto, a myth symbolizing the springing of the corn from the earth in the springtime.

In doubtful dreams of dreams;
I watch the green field growing
For reaping folk and sowing,
For harvest-time and mowing,
 A sleepy world of streams.

I am tired of tears and laughter,
 And men that laugh and weep;
Of what may come hereafter
 For men that sow to reap:
I am weary of days and hours,
Blown buds of barren flowers,
Desires and dreams and powers
 And everything but sleep.

Here life has death for neighbour,
 And far from eye or ear
Wan waves and wet winds labour,
 Weak ships and spirits steer;
They drive adrift, and whither
They wot not who make thither;
But no such winds blow hither,
 And no such things grow here.

No growth of moor or coppice,
 No heather-flower or vine,
But bloomless buds of poppies,
 Green grapes of Proserpine,
Pale beds of blowing rushes,
Where no leaf blooms or blushes
Save this whereout she crushes
 For dead men deadly wine.

Pale, without name or number,
 In fruitless fields of corn,
They bow themselves and slumber
 All night till light is born;
And like a soul belated,
In hell and heaven unmated,
By cloud and mist abated
 Comes out of darkness morn.

Though one were strong as seven,
   He too with death shall dwell,
Nor wake with wings in heaven,
   Nor weep for pains in hell;
Though one were fair as roses,   45
His beauty clouds and closes;
And well though love reposes,
   In the end it is not well.

Pale, beyond porch and portal,
   Crowned with calm leaves, she stands   50
Who gathers all things mortal
   With cold immortal hands;
Her languid lips are sweeter
Than love's who fears to greet her,
To men that mix and meet her   55
   From many times and lands.

She waits for each and other,
   She waits for all men born;
Forgets the earth her mother,
   The life of fruits and corn;   60
And spring and seed and swallow
Take wing for her and follow
Where summer song rings hollow
   And flowers are put to scorn.

There go the loves that wither,   65
   The old loves with wearier wings;
And all dead years draw thither,
   And all disastrous things;
Dead dreams of days forsaken,
Blind buds that snows have shaken,   70
Wild leaves that winds have taken,
   Red strays of ruined springs.

We are not sure of sorrow,
   And joy was never sure;
Today will die tomorrow;   75

Time stoops to no man's lure;
And love, grown faint and fretful,
With lips but half regretful
Sighs, and with eyes forgetful
80   Weeps that no loves endure.

From too much love of living,
    From hope and fear set free,
We thank with brief thanksgiving
    Whatever gods may be
85 That no life lives for ever;
    That dead men rise up never;
    That even the weariest river
        Winds somewhere safe to sea.

Then star nor sun shall waken,
90   Nor any change of light:
Nor sound of waters shaken,
    Nor any sound or sight:
Nor wintry leaves nor vernal,
Nor days nor things diurnal;
95 Only the sleep eternal
    In an eternal night.

THOMAS HARDY *1840-1928*

81 *1 The Darkling Thrush*

DECEMBER 1900

I leant upon a coppice gate
    When Frost was spectre-gray,
And Winter's dregs made desolate
    The weakening eye of day.
5   The tangled bine-stems scored the sky
    Like strings of broken lyres,
And all mankind that haunted nigh
    Had sought their household fires.

140

The land's sharp features seemed to be
    The Century's corpse outleant,   10
His crypt the cloudy canopy,
    The wind his death lament.
The ancient pulse of germ and birth
    Was shrunken hard and dry,
And every spirit upon earth   15
    Seemed fervourless as I.

At once a voice arose among
    The bleak twigs overhead
In a full-hearted evensong
    Of joy illimited;   20
An aged thrush, frail, gaunt, and small,
    In blast-beruffled plume,
Had chosen thus to fling his soul
    Upon the growing gloom.

So little cause for carollings   25
    Of such ecstatic sound
Was written on terrestrial things
    Afar or nigh around,
That I could think there trembled through
    His happy good-night air   30
Some blessed Hope, whereof he knew
    And I was unaware.

82 ⋌ The Convergence of the Twain
Lines on the Loss of the "Titanic"

I

In a solitude of the sea
    Deep from human vanity,
And the Pride of Life that planned her, stilly couches she.

II

Steel chambers, late the pyres
    Of her salamandrine fires,
Cold currents thrid, and turn to rhythmic tidal lyres.

Over the mirrors meant
To glass the opulent
The sea-worm crawls—grotesque, slimed, dumb, indifferent.

IV

Jewels in joy designed
To ravish the sensuous mind
Lie lightless, all their sparkles bleared and black and blind.

V

Dim moon-eyed fishes near
Gaze at the gilded gear
And query: "What does this vaingloriousness down here?"

VI

Well: while was fashioning
This creature of cleaving wing,
The Immanent Will that stirs and urges everything

VII

Prepared a sinister mate
For her—so gaily great—
A Shape of Ice, for the time far and dissociate.

VIII

And as the smart ship grew
In stature, grace, and hue,
In shadowy silent distance grew the Iceberg too.

IX

Alien they seemed to be;
No mortal eye could see
The intimate welding of their later history,

X

Or sign that they were bent
By paths coincident
On being anon twin halves of one august event,

XI

Till the Spinner of the Years
    Said "Now!" And each one hears,
And consummation comes, and jars two hemispheres.

GERARD MANLEY HOPKINS *1844-1889*

83   *The Windhover*

TO CHRIST OUR LORD

I caught this morning morning's minion, king-
        dom of daylight's dauphin, dapple-dawn-drawn Falcon,
        in his riding
    Of the rolling level underneath him steady air, and
        striding
High there, how he rung upon the rein of a wimpling wing
In his ecstasy! then off, off forth on swing,   5
    As a skate's heel sweeps smooth on a bow-bend: the
        hurl and gliding
    Rebuffed the big wind. My heart in hiding
Stirred for a bird,—the achieve of, the mastery of the thing!

Brute beauty and valour and act, oh, air, pride, plume, here
    Buckle! AND the fire that breaks from thee then, a billion   10
Times told lovelier, more dangerous, O my chevalier!

    No wonder of it: shéer plód makes plow down sillion
Shine, and blue-bleak embers, ah my dear,
    Fall, gall themselves, and gash gold-vermilion.

The Windhover: the kestrel or falcon.
   1. *minion:* little darling.
   2. *dauphin:* young prince (a name given to the heir apparent to the French
      throne in medieval times).
   4. *rung upon the rein:* the image is of a horse circling round its trainer at the
      end of a long rein.   *wimpling:* rippling.
  10. *Buckle:* has two meanings at once as applied to the bird and to the poet's
      heart: (1) clasp, fasten or buckle together; (2) bend, crumple, collapse.
  11. *chevalier:* lord, knight, master. Note that all these words have a connotation
      of medieval romance and courtly chivalry.
  12. *sillion:* furrow of ploughed earth.

84 *1 To an Athlete Dying Young*

The time you won your town the race
We chaired you through the market-place;
Man and boy stood cheering by,
And home we brought you shoulder-high.

5 Today, the road all runners come,
Shoulder-high we bring you home,
And set you at your threshold down,
Townsman of a stiller town.

Smart lad, to slip betimes away
10 From fields where glory does not stay,
And early though the laurel grows
It withers quicker than the rose.

Eyes the shady night has shut
Cannot see the record cut,
15 And silence sounds no worse than cheers
After earth has stopped the ears:

Now you will not swell the rout
Of lads that wore their honors out,
Runners whom renown outran
20 And the name died before the man.

So set, before its echoes fade,
The fleet foot on the sill of shade,
And hold to the low lintel up
The still-defended challenge-cup.

25 And round that early-laureled head
Will flock to gaze the strengthless dead,
And find unwithered on its curls
The garland briefer than a girl's.

85 ⸱ *Leda and the Swan*

A sudden blow: the great wings beating still
Above the staggering girl, her thighs caressed
By the dark webs, her nape caught in his bill,
He holds her helpless breast upon his breast.

How can those terrified vague fingers push   5
The feathered glory from her loosening thighs?
And how can body, laid in that white rush,
But feel the strange heart beating where it lies?

A shudder in the loins engenders there
The broken wall, the burning roof and tower   10
And Agamemnon dead.
                         Being so caught up,
So mastered by the brute blood of the air,
Did she put on his knowledge with his power
Before the indifferent beak could let her drop?

86 ⸱ *The Second Coming*

Turning and turning in the widening gyre
The falcon cannot hear the falconer;
Things fall apart; the center cannot hold;

Leda and the Swan: Leda, wife of Tyndarus, king of Sparta, was seen bathing in a stream by Zeus, who took the form of a swan in order to ravish her. She bore him the twins Castor and Pollux and Helen, for whose sake the Trojan war was later fought. All the tragic events of the future—the abduction of Helen, the ten years' siege of Troy, and the return to Greece of King Agamemnon to be murdered by his wife Clytemnestra—are seen here as already existing as potentialities in the rape of Leda.

The Second Coming: Christ's prophecy (Matthew 24) and the sphinx-like beast which is Antichrist in the Apocalypse are here fused in a prophecy of a new cycle (gyre) of history that will inaugurate a second double millennium of barbaric chaos to succeed the Christian era.

2. *falcon:* the subject who owes obedience to a king or other legitimate source of authority (the Falconer) or man who owes obedience to God or Christ.

Mere anarchy is loosed upon the world,
The blood-dimmed tide is loosed, and everywhere
The ceremony of innocence is drowned;
The best lack all conviction, while the worst
Are full of passionate intensity.

Surely some revelation is at hand;
Surely the Second Coming is at hand.
The Second Coming! Hardly are those words out
When a vast image out of *Spiritus Mundi*
Troubles my sight: somewhere in sands of the desert
A shape with lion body and the head of a man,
A gaze blank and pitiless as the sun,
Is moving its slow thighs, while all about it
Reel shadows of the indignant desert birds.

The darkness drops again; but now I know
That twenty centuries of stony sleep
Were vexed to nightmare by a rocking cradle,
And what rough beast, its hour come round at last,
Slouches towards Bethlehem to be born?

87 ┐ *Sailing to Byzantium*

That is no country for old men. The young
In one another's arms, birds in the trees
—Those dying generations—at their song,
The salmon-falls, the mackerel-crowded seas,
Fish, flesh, or fowl, commend all summer long
Whatever is begotten, born, and dies.
Caught in that sensual music all neglect
Monuments of unaging intellect.

12. *Spiritus Mundi: anima mundi,* world soul, world mind, a name Yeats found
in the writings of Henry More, a seventeenth century English platonist, which
stands for a kind of racial memory and accounts for the recurrence of similar
myths in unrelated cultures. It has a close affinity with what the psychologist
Jung names the Collective Unconscious.

An aged man is but a paltry thing,
A tattered coat upon a stick, unless   10
Soul clap its hands and sing, and louder sing
For every tatter in its mortal dress,
Nor is there singing school but studying
Monuments of its own magnificence;
And therefore I have sailed the seas and come   15
To the holy city of Byzantium.

O sages standing in God's holy fire
As in the gold mosaic of a wall,
Come from the holy fire, perne in a gyre,
And be the singing-masters of my soul.   20
Consume my heart away; sick with desire
And fastened to a dying animal
It knows not what it is; and gather me
Into the artifice of eternity.

Once out of nature I shall never take   25
My bodily form from any natural thing,
But such a form as Grecian goldsmiths make
Of hammered gold and gold enameling
To keep a drowsy Emperor awake;
Or set upon a golden bough to sing   30
To lords and ladies of Byzantium
Of what is past, or passing, or to come.

16. *the holy city of Byzantium:* Constantinople, the symbol of a civilization at its height at the end of the first millennium of the Christian era, a meeting point of Eastern and Western religion, whose art, as represented by the gold mosaics of the Cathedral of Santa Sophia, was metallic, nonrepresentational, and (in Yeats's view) superhuman. Here it symbolizes a state of mind or being made possible by the creative imagination of the artist.

19. *perne:* an Irish dialect word meaning a spool or bobbin on which a thread is wound.   *gyre:* a swooping whirling circular motion.

25-32. Yeats adds a note: "I have read somewhere that in the Emperor's palace at Byzantium was a tree made of gold and silver, and artificial birds that sang."

88 / *Mr. Flood's Party*

    Old Eben Flood, climbing alone one night
    Over the hill between the town below
    And the forsaken upland hermitage
    That held as much as he should ever know
5   On earth again of home, paused warily.
    The road was his with not a native near;
    And Eben, having leisure, said aloud,
    For no man else in Tilbury Town to hear:

    "Well, Mr. Flood, we have the harvest moon
10   Again, and we may not have many more;
    The bird is on the wing, the poet says,
    And you and I have said it here before.
    Drink to the bird." He raised up to the light
    The jug that he had gone so far to fill,
15   And answered huskily: "Well, Mr. Flood,
    Since you propose it, I believe I will."

    Alone, as if enduring to the end
    A valiant armor of scarred hopes outworn,
    He stood there in the middle of the road
20   Like Roland's ghost winding a silent horn.
    Below him, in the town among the trees,
    Where friends of other days had honored him,
    A phantom salutation of the dead
    Rang thinly till old Eben's eyes were dim.

25   Then, as a mother lays her sleeping child
    Down tenderly, fearing it may awake,
    He set the jug down slowly at his feet
    With trembling care, knowing that most things break;
    And only when assured that on firm earth
30   It stood, as the uncertain lives of men
    Assuredly did not, he paced away,
    And with his hand extended paused again:

"Well, Mr. Flood, we have not met like this
In a long time; and many a change has come
To both of us, I fear, since last it was   35
We had a drop together. Welcome home!"
Convivially returning with himself,
Again he raised the jug up to the light
And with an acquiescent quaver said:
"Well, Mr. Flood, if you insist, I might.   40

"Only a very little, Mr. Flood—
For auld lang syne. No more, sir; that will do."
So, for the time, apparently it did,
And Eben evidently thought so too;
For soon amid the silver loneliness   45
Of night he lifted up his voice and sang,
Secure, with only two moons listening,
Until the whole harmonious landscape rang—

"For auld lang syne." The weary throat gave out,
The last word wavered; and the song being done,   50
He raised again the jug regretfully
And shook his head, and was again alone.
There was not much that was ahead of him,
And there was nothing in the town below—
Where strangers would have shut the many doors   55
That many friends had opened long ago.

WALTER DE LA MARE 1873-1956

89 ⟋ The Listeners

"Is there anybody there?" said the Traveller,
    Knocking on the moonlit door;
And his horse in the silence champed the grasses
    Of the forest's ferny floor:
And a bird flew up out of the turret,   5
    Above the Traveller's head:

149

And he smote upon the door again a second time;
  "Is there anybody there?" he said.
But no one descended to the Traveller;
  No head from the leaf-fringed sill
10
Leaned over and looked into his grey eyes,
  Where he stood perplexed and still.
But only a host of phantom listeners
  That dwelt in the lone house then
15
Stood listening in the quiet of the moonlight
  To that voice from the world of men:
Stood thronging the faint moonbeams on the dark stair,
  That goes down to the empty hall,
Hearkening in an air stirred and shaken
20
  By the lonely Traveller's call.
And he felt in his heart their strangeness,
  Their stillness answering his cry,
While his horse moved, cropping the dark turf,
  'Neath the starred and leafy sky;
25
For he suddenly smote on the door, even
  Louder, and lifted his head:—
"Tell them I came, and no one answered,
  That I kept my word!" he said.
30
Never the least stir made the listeners,
  Though every word he spake
Fell echoing through the shadowiness of the still house
  From the one man left awake;
Ay, they heard his foot upon the stirrup,
  And the sound of iron on stone,
35
And how the silence surged softly backward,
  When the plunging hoofs were gone.

ROBERT FROST *1875-1963*

90   *Two Look at Two*

  Love and forgetting might have carried them
  A little further up the mountain side
  With night so near, but not much further up.

They must have halted soon in any case
With thoughts of the path back, how rough it was   5
With rock and washout, and unsafe in darkness;
When they were halted by a tumbled wall
With barbed-wire binding. They stood facing this,
Spending what onward impulse they still had
In one last look the way they must not go,   10
On up the failing path, where, if a stone
Or earthslide moved at night, it moved itself;
No footstep moved it. "This is all," they sighed,
"Good-night to woods." But not so; there was more.
A doe from round a spruce stood looking at them   15
Across the wall as near the wall as they.
She saw them in their field, they her in hers.
The difficulty of seeing what stood still,
Like some up-ended bowlder split in two,
Was in her clouded eyes: they saw no fear there.   20
She seemed to think that two thus they were safe.
Then, as if they were something that, though strange,
She could not trouble her mind with too long,
She sighed and passed unscared along the wall.
"*This,* then, is all. What more is there to ask?"   25
But no, not yet. A snort to bid them wait.
A buck from round the spruce stood looking at them
Across the wall, as near the wall as they.
This was an antlered buck of lusty nostril,
Not the same doe come back into her place.   30
He viewed them quizzically with jerks of head,
As if to ask, "Why don't you make some motion?
Or give some sign of life? Because you can't.
I doubt if you're as living as you look."
Thus till he had them almost feeling dared   35
To stretch a proffering hand—and a spell-breaking.
Then he too passed unscared along the wall.
Two had seen two, whichever side you spoke from.
"This *must* be all." It was all. Still they stood,
A great wave from it going over them,   40
As if the earth in one unlooked-for favor
Had made them certain earth returned their love.

She is as in a field a silken tent
At midday when a sunny summer breeze
Has dried the dew and all its ropes relent,
So that in guys it gently sways at ease,
5   And its supporting central cedar pole,
That is its pinnacle to heavenward
And signifies the sureness of the soul,
Seems to owe naught to any single cord,
But strictly held by none, is loosely bound
10   By countless silken ties of love and thought
To everything on earth the compass round,
And only by one's going slightly taut
In the capriciousness of summer air
Is of the slightest bondage made aware.

92 1 *Directive*

Back out of all this now too much for us,
Back in a time made simple by the loss
Of detail, burned, dissolved, and broken off
Like a graveyard marble sculpture in the weather,
5   There is a house that is no more a house
Upon a farm that is no more a farm
And in a town that is no more a town.
The road there, if you'll let a guide direct you
Who only has at heart your getting lost,
10   May seem as if it should have been a quarry—
Great monolithic knees the former town
Long since gave up pretence of keeping covered.
And there's a story in a book about it:
Besides the wear of iron wagon wheels
15   The ledges show lines ruled southeast northwest,
The chisel work of an enormous Glacier
That braced his feet against the Arctic Pole.
You must not mind a certain coolness from him
Still said to haunt this side of Panther Mountain.

Nor need you mind the serial ordeal   20
Of being watched from forty cellar holes
As if by eye pairs out of forty firkins.
As for the woods' excitement over you
That sends light rustle rushes to their leaves,
Charge that to upstart inexperience.   25
Where were they all not twenty years ago?
They think too much of having shaded out
A few old pecker-fretted apple trees.
Make yourself up a cheering song of how
Someone's road home from work this once was,   30
Who may be just ahead of you on foot
Or creaking with a buggy load of grain.
The height of the adventure is the height
Of country where two village cultures faded
Into each other. Both of them are lost.   35
And if you're lost enough to find yourself
By now, pull in your ladder road behind you
And put a sign up CLOSED to all but me.
Then make yourself at home. The only field
Now left's no bigger than a harness gall.   40
First there's the children's house of make-believe,
Some shattered dishes underneath a pine,
The playthings in the playhouse of the children.
Weep for what little things could make them glad.
Then for the house that is no more a house,   45
But only a belilaced cellar hole,
Now slowly closing like a dent in dough.
This was no playhouse but a house in earnest.
Your destination and your destiny's
A brook that was the water of the house,   50
Cold as a spring as yet so near its source,
Too lofty and original to rage.
(We know the valley streams that when aroused
Will leave their tatters hung on barb and thorn.)
I have kept hidden in the instep arch   55
Of an old cedar at the waterside
A broken drinking goblet like the Grail
Under a spell so the wrong ones can't find it,

So can't get saved, as Saint Mark says they mustn't.
60   (I stole the goblet from the children's playhouse.)
Here are your waters and your watering place.
Drink and be whole again beyond confusion.

WALLACE STEVENS *1879-1955*

93 *1 Sunday Morning*

I

Complacencies of the peignoir, and late
Coffee and oranges in a sunny chair,
And the green freedom of a cockatoo
Upon a rug mingle to dissipate
5   The holy hush of ancient sacrifice.
She dreams a little, and she feels the dark
Encroachment of that old catastrophe,
As a calm darkens among water-lights.
The pungent oranges and bright, green wings
10   Seem things in some procession of the dead,
Winding across wide water, without sound.
The day is like wide water, without sound,
Stilled for the passing of her dreaming feet
Over the seas, to silent Palestine,
15   Dominion of the blood and sepulchre.

II

Why should she give her bounty to the dead?
What is divinity if it can come
Only in silent shadows and in dreams?
Shall she not find in comforts of the sun,
20   In pungent fruit and bright, green wings, or else
In any balm or beauty of the earth,
Things to be cherished like the thought of heaven?
Divinity must live within herself:

59. *Saint Mark:* See Mark 4:11-12, where Christ declares he speaks in parables
(as Frost in this poem) so that only those worthy to be saved should under-
stand the real significance of his message.

Passions of rain, or moods in falling snow;
Grievings in loneliness, or unsubdued   25
Elations when the forest blooms; gusty
Emotions on wet roads on autumn nights;
All pleasures and all pains, remembering
The bough of summer and the winter branch.
These are the measures destined for her soul.   30

III

Jove in the clouds had his inhuman birth.
No mother suckled him, no sweet land gave
Large-mannered motions to his mythy mind.
He moved among us, as a muttering king,
Magnificent, would move among his hinds,   35
Until our blood, commingling, virginal,
With heaven, brought such requital to desire
The very hinds discerned it in a star.
Shall our blood fail? Or shall it come to be
The blood of paradise? And shall the earth   40
Seem all of paradise that we shall know?
The sky will be much friendlier then than now,
A part of labor and a part of pain,
And next in glory to enduring love,
Not this dividing and indifferent blue.   45

IV

She says, "I am content when wakened birds,
Before they fly, test the reality
Of misty fields, by their sweet questionings;
But when the birds are gone, and their warm fields
Return no more, where, then, is paradise?"   50
There is not any haunt of prophecy,
Nor any old chimera of the grave,
Neither the golden underground, nor isle
Melodious, where spirits gat them home,
Nor visionary south, nor cloudy palm   55
Remote on heaven's hill, that has endured
As April's green endures; or will endure
Like her remembrance of awakened birds,

Or her desire for June and evening, tipped
60   By the consummation of the swallow's wings.

                              V

She says, "But in contentment I still feel
The need of some imperishable bliss."
Death is the mother of beauty; hence from her,
Alone, shall come fulfilment to our dreams
65   And our desires. Although she strews the leaves
Of sure obliteration on our paths,
The path sick sorrow took, the many paths
Where triumph rang its brassy phrase, or love
Whispered a little out of tenderness,
70   She makes the willow shiver in the sun
For maidens who were wont to sit and gaze
Upon the grass, relinquished to their feet.
She causes boys to pile new plums and pears
On disregarded plate. The maidens taste
75   And stray impassioned in the littering leaves.

                              VI

Is there no change of death in paradise?
Does ripe fruit never fall? Or do the boughs
Hang always heavy in that perfect sky,
Unchanging, yet so like our perishing earth,
80   With rivers like our own that seek for seas
They never find, the same receding shores
That never touch with inarticulate pang?
Why set the pear upon those river-banks
Or spice the shores with odors of the plum?
85   Alas, that they should wear our colors there,
The silken weavings of our afternoons,
And pick the strings of our insipid lutes!
Death is the mother of beauty, mystical,
Within whose burning bosom we devise
90   Our earthly mothers waiting, sleeplessly.

                              VII

Supple and turbulent, a ring of men
Shall chant in orgy on a summer morn

                            156

Their boisterous devotion to the sun,
Not as a god, but as a god might be,
Naked among them, like a savage source. 95
Their chant shall be a chant of paradise,
Out of their blood, returning to the sky;
And in their chant shall enter, voice by voice,
The windy lake wherein their lord delights,
The trees, like serafin, and echoing hills, 100
That choir among themselves long afterward.
They shall know well the heavenly fellowship
Of men that perish and of summer morn.
And whence they came and whither they shall go
The dew upon their feet shall manifest. 105

VIII

She hears, upon that water without sound,
A voice that cries, "The tomb in Palestine
Is not the porch of spirits lingering.
It is the grave of Jesus, where he lay."
We live in an old chaos of the sun, 110
Or old dependency of day and night,
Or island solitude, unsponsored, free,
Of that wide water, inescapable.
Deer walk upon our mountains, and the quail
Whistle about us their spontaneous cries; 115
Sweet berries ripen in the wilderness;
And, in the isolation of the sky,
At evening, casual flocks of pigeons make
Ambiguous undulations as they sink,
Downward to darkness, on extended wings. 120

WILLIAM CARLOS WILLIAMS 1883-1963

94 ⸱ The Yachts

contend in a sea which the land partly encloses
shielding them from the too heavy blows
of an ungoverned ocean which when it chooses

tortures the biggest hulls, the best man knows
to pit against its beatings, and sinks them pitilessly.
Mothlike in mists, scintillant in the minute

brilliance of cloudless days, with broad bellying sails
they glide to the wind tossing green water
from their sharp prows while over them the crew crawls

ant-like, solicitously grooming them, releasing,
making fast as they turn, lean far over and having
caught the wind again, side by side, head for the mark.

In a well guarded arena of open water surrounded by
lesser and greater craft which, sycophant, lumbering
and flittering follow them, they appear youthful, rare

as the light of a happy eye, live with the grace
of all that in the mind is fleckless, free and
naturally to be desired. Now the sea which holds them

is moody, lapping their glossy sides, as if feeling
for some slightest flaw but fails completely.
Today no race. Then the wind comes again. The yachts

move, jockeying for a start, the signal is set and they
are off. Now the waves strike at them but they are too
well made, they slip through, though they take in canvas.

Arms with hands grasping seek to clutch at the prows.
Bodies thrown recklessly in the way are cut aside.
It is a sea of faces about them in agony, in despair

until the horror of the race dawns staggering the mind,
the whole sea become an entanglement of watery bodies
lost to the world bearing what they cannot hold. Broken,

beaten, desolate, reaching from the dead to be taken up
they cry out, failing, failing! their cries rising
in waves still as the skillful yachts pass over.

95 ⸻ The Seafarer

FROM THE ANGLO-SAXON

May I for my own self song's truth reckon,
Journey's jargon, how I in harsh days
Hardship endured oft.
Bitter breast-cares have I abided,
Known on my keel many a care's hold,   5
And dire sea-surge, and there I oft spent
Narrow nightwatch nigh the ship's head
While she tossed close to cliffs. Coldly afflicted,
My feet were by frost benumbed.
Chill its chains are; chafing sighs   10
Hew my heart round and hunger begot
Mere-weary mood. Lest man know not
That he on dry land loveliest liveth,
List how I, care-wretched, on ice-cold sea,
Weathered the winter, wretched outcast   15
Deprived of my kinsmen;
Hung with hard ice-flakes, where hail-scur flew,
There I heard naught save the harsh sea
And ice-cold wave, at whiles the swan cries,
Did for my games the gannet's clamour,   20
Sea-fowls' loudness was for me laughter,
The mews' singing all my mead-drink.
Storms, on the stone-cliffs beaten, fell on the stern
In icy feathers; full oft the eagle screamed
With spray on his pinion.   25
                          Not any protector
May make merry man faring needy.
This he little believes, who aye in winsome life
Abides 'mid burghers some heavy business,
Wealthy and wine-flushed, how I weary oft   30
Must bide above brine.
Neareth nightshade, snoweth from north,
Frost froze the land, hail fell on earth then,
Corn of the coldest. Nathless there knocketh now

35 The heart's thought that I on high streams
   The salt-wavy tumult traverse alone.
   Moaneth alway my mind's lust
   That I fare forth, that I afar hence
   Seek out a foreign fastness.
40 For this there's no mood-lofty man over earth's midst,
   Not though he be given his good, but will have in his youth greed;
   Nor his deed to the daring, nor his king to the faithful
   But shall have his sorrow for sea-fare
   Whatever his lord will.
45 He hath not heart for harping, nor in ring-having
   Nor winsomeness to wife, nor world's delight
   Nor any whit else save the wave's slash,
   Yet longing comes upon him to fare forth on the water.
   Bosque taketh blossom, cometh beauty of berries,
50 Fields to fairness, land fares brisker,
   All this admonisheth man eager of mood,
   The heart turns to travel so that he then thinks
   On flood-ways to be far departing.
   Cuckoo calleth with gloomy crying,
55 He singeth summerward, bodeth sorrow,
   The bitter heart's blood. Burgher knows not—
   He the prosperous man—what some perform
   Where wandering them widest draweth.
   So that but now my heart burst from my breastlock,
60 My mood 'mid the mere-flood,
   Over the whale's acre, would wander wide.
   On earth's shelter cometh oft to me,
   Eager and ready, the crying lone-flyer,
   Whets for the whale-path the heart irresistibly,
65 O'er tracks of ocean; seeing that anyhow
   My lord deems to me this dead life
   On loan and on land, I believe not
   That any earth-weal eternal standeth
   Save there be somewhat calamitous
70 That, ere a man's tide go, turn it to twain.
   Disease or oldness or sword-hate
   Beats out the breath from doom-gripped body.
   And for this, every earl whatever, for those speaking after—
   Laud of the living, boasteth some last word,

That he will work ere he pass onward,   75
Frame on the fair earth 'gainst foes his malice,
Daring ado, . . .
So that all men shall honour him after
And his laud beyond them remain 'mid the English,
Aye, for ever, a lasting life's-blast,   80
Delight 'mid the doughty.
                                        Days little durable
And all arrogance of earthen riches,
There come now no kings nor Caesars
Nor gold-giving lords like those gone.   85
Howe'er in mirth most magnified,
Whoe'er lived in life most lordliest,
Drear all this excellence, delights undurable!
Waneth the watch, but the world holdeth.
Tomb hideth trouble. The blade is layed low.   90
Earthly glory ageth and seareth.
No man at all going the earth's gait,
But age fares against him, his face paleth,
Grey-haired he groaneth, knows gone companions,
Lordly men, are to earth o'ergiven,   95
Nor may he then the flesh-cover, whose life ceaseth,
Nor eat the sweet nor feel the sorry,
Nor stir hand nor think in mid heart,
And though he strew the grave with gold,
His born brothers, their buried bodies   100
Be an unlikely treasure hoard.

                        T. S. ELIOT 1888-1965

96 ⟡ *Gerontion*

                    Thou hast nor youth nor age
                But as it were an after dinner sleep
                        Dreaming of both.

        Here I am, an old man in a dry month,
        Being read to by a boy, waiting for rain.

Gerontion: oldness, or the spirit of old age. The old man whose interior monologue
we listen to symbolizes the spirit of decadence in an age or a culture.
Thou hast nor youth nor age, etc.: Shakespeare, *Measure for Measure*, III, i.

I was neither at the hot gates
Nor fought in the warm rain
5   Nor knee deep in the salt marsh, heaving a cutlass,
Bitten by flies, fought.
My house is a decayed house,
And the jew squats on the window sill, the owner,
Spawned in some estaminet of Antwerp,
10   Blistered in Brussels, patched and peeled in London.
The goat coughs at night in the field overhead;
Rocks, moss, stonecrop, iron, merds.
The woman keeps the kitchen, makes tea,
Sneezes at evening, poking the peevish gutter.
                            I an old man,
15   A dull head among windy spaces.

Signs are taken for wonders. "We would see a sign!"
The word within a word, unable to speak a word,
Swaddled with darkness. In the juvescence of the year
Came Christ the tiger

20   In depraved May, dogwood and chestnut, flowering judas,
To be eaten, to be divided, to be drunk
Among whispers; by Mr. Silvero
With caressing hands, at Limoges
Who walked all night in the next room;
25   By Hakagawa, bowing among the Titians;
By Madame de Tornquist, in the dark room
Shifting the candles; Fräulein von Kulp
Who turned in the hall, one hand on the door. Vacant shuttles
Weave the wind. I have no ghosts,

3. *hot gates:* English translation of Thermopylae, the pass where three hundred Spartans under Leonidas sacrificed their lives to delay the invading Persians in 480 B.C. The reference here is symbolic of heroic action in the distant past.

16. *"We would see a sign":* the demand of the sceptical Pharisees, who wished Christ to prove his divinity by a miracle.

17. *The word within a word,* etc.: A quotation from a Christmas sermon preached by Lancelot Andrewes in 1622 before King James I. It might be paraphrased as: "The word of God—that is, God himself—within the word *Christ,* who as an infant could not yet speak a word. This is a striking example of the serious use of the pun.

An old man in a draughty house   30
Under a windy knob.

After such knowledge, what forgiveness? Think now
History has many cunning passages, contrived corridors
And issues, deceives with whispering ambitions,
Guides us by vanities. Think now   35
She gives when our attention is distracted
And what she gives, gives with such supple confusions
That the giving famishes the craving. Gives too late
What's not believed in, or if still believed,
In memory only, reconsidered passion. Gives too soon   40
Into weak hands, what's thought can be dispensed with
Till the refusal propagates a fear. Think
Neither fear nor courage saves us. Unnatural vices
Are fathered by our heroism. Virtues
Are forced upon us by our impudent crimes.   45
These tears are shaken from the wrath-bearing tree.

The tiger springs in the new year. Us he devours. Think at last
We have not reached conclusion, when I
Stiffen in a rented house. Think at last
I have not made this show purposelessly   50
And it is not by any concitation
Of the backward devils.
I would meet you upon this honestly.
I that was near your heart was removed therefrom
To lose beauty in terror, terror in inquisition.   55
I have lost my passion: why should I need to keep it
Since what is kept must be adulterated?
I have lost my sight, smell, hearing, taste, and touch:
How should I use them for your closer contact?

These with a thousand small deliberations   60
Protract the profit of their chilled delirium,
Excite the membrane, when the sense has cooled,
With pungent sauces, multiply variety
In a wilderness of mirrors. What will the spider do,
Suspend its operations, will the weevil   65
Delay? De Bailhache, Fresca, Mrs. Cammel, whirled

163

Beyond the circuit of the shuddering Bear
In fractured atoms. Gull against the wind, in the windy straits
Of Belle Isle, or running on the Horn,
70   White feathers in the snow, the Gulf claims,
And an old man driven by the Trades
To a sleepy corner.

                                    Tenants of the house,
Thoughts of a dry brain in a dry season.

97 ⸱ *The Hollow Men*

MISTAH KURTZ—HE DEAD.

A penny for the Old Guy

I

We are the hollow men
We are the stuffed men
Leaning together
Headpiece filled with straw. Alas!
5   Our dried voices, when
We whisper together
Are quiet and meaningless
As wind in dry grass
Or rats' feet over broken glass
10   In our dry cellar

Shape without form, shade without colour,
Paralysed force, gesture without motion;

Those who have crossed
With direct eyes, to death's other Kingdom
15   Remember us—if at all—not as lost
Violent souls, but only
As the hollow men
The stuffed men.

164

II

Eyes I dare not meet in dreams
In death's dream kingdom   20
These do not appear:
There, the eyes are
Sunlight on a broken column
There, is a tree swinging
And voices are   25
In the wind's singing
More distant and more solemn
Than a fading star.

Let me be no nearer
In death's dream kingdom   30
Let me also wear
Such deliberate disguises
Rat's coat, crowskin, crossed staves
In a field
Behaving as the wind behaves   35
No nearer—

Not that final meeting
In the twilight kingdom

III

This is the dead land
This is cactus land   40
Here the stone images
Are raised, here they receive
The supplication of a dead man's hand
Under the twinkle of a fading star.

Is it like this   45
In death's other kingdom
Waking alone
At the hour when we are
Trembling with tenderness
Lips that would kiss   50
Form prayers to broken stone.

The eyes are not here
There are no eyes here
In this valley of dying stars
55 In this hollow valley
This broken jaw of our lost kingdoms

In this last of meeting places
We grope together
And avoid speech
60 Gathered on this beach of the tumid river

Sightless, unless
The eyes reappear
As the perpetual star
Multifoliate rose
65 Of death's twilight kingdom
The hope only
Of empty men.

V

Here we go round the prickly pear
Prickly pear prickly pear
70 *Here we go round the prickly pear*
At five o'clock in the morning.

Between the idea
And the reality
Between the motion
75 And the act
Falls the Shadow

For Thine is the Kingdom

Between the conception
And the creation
80 Between the emotion
And the response
Falls the Shadow

Life is very long

Between the desire
And the spasm   85
Between the potency
And the existence
Between the essence
And the descent
Falls the Shadow   90

For Thine is the Kingdom

For Thine is
Life is
For Thine is the

This is the way the world ends   95
This is the way the world ends
This is the way the world ends
Not with a bang but a whimper.

W. H. AUDEN   *1907-*

98 ↑ September 1, 1939

I sit in one of the dives
On Fifty-Second Street
Uncertain and afraid
As the clever hopes expire
Of a low dishonest decade: 5
Waves of anger and fear
Circulate over the bright
And darkened lands of the earth,
Obsessing our private lives;
The unmentionable odour of death   10
Offends the September night.

September 1, 1939: the date of the outbreak of World War II.

167

Accurate scholarship can
Unearth the whole offence
From Luther until now
That has driven a culture mad,
Find what occurred at Linz,
What huge imago made
A psychopathic god:
I and the public know
What all schoolchildren learn,
Those to whom evil is done
Do evil in return.

Exiled Thucydides knew
All that a speech can say
About Democracy,
And what dictators do,
The elderly rubbish they talk
To an apathetic grave;
Analysed all in his book,
The enlightenment driven away,
The habit-forming pain,
Mismanagement and grief:
We must suffer them all again.

Into this neutral air
Where blind skyscrapers use
Their full height to proclaim
The strength of Collective Man,
Each language pours its vain
Competitive excuse:

14. *Luther:* the German Protestant Reformation is here viewed as the beginning of a revolt against international order and authority that led finally to the national barbarism of Nazi Germany.

16. *what occurred at Linz:* the Austrian Chancellor met Hitler at Linz in March, 1938, and was forced to sign the agreement by which Germany annexed Austria.

23-33. The great Greek historian, Thucydides, exiled for failure as a naval commander in the war against Sparta. His history gives an imaginative recreation of Pericles' speech honoring the war dead, which contains a glowing celebration of Athenian democracy, and recounts the gradual decay of Athenian morality under the impact of war after the death of Pericles.

24. *speech:* the famous funeral oration of Pericles.

But who can live for long   40
In an euphoric dream;
Out of the mirror they stare,
Imperialism's face
And the international wrong.

Faces along the bar   45
Cling to their average day:
The lights must never go out,
The music must always play,
All the conventions conspire
To make this fort assume   50
The furniture of home;
Lest we should see where we are,
Lost in a haunted wood,
Children afraid of the night
Who have never been happy or good.   55

The windiest militant trash
Important Persons shout
It is not so crude as our wish:
What mad Nijinsky wrote
About Diaghilev   .   60
Is true of the normal heart;
For the error bred in the bone
Of each woman and each man
Craves what it cannot have,
Not universal love   65
But to be loved alone.

From the conservative dark
Into the ethical life
The dense commuters come,
Repeating their morning vow;   70
"I *will* be true to the wife,
I'll concentrate more on my work,"
And helpless governors wake
To resume their compulsory game:
Who can release them now,   75
Who can reach the deaf,
Who can speak for the dumb?

169

All I have is a voice
To undo the folded lie,
80 The romantic lie in the brain
Of the sensual man-in-the-street
And the lie of Authority
Whose buildings grope the sky:
There is no such thing as the State
85 And no one exists alone;
Hunger allows no choice
To the citizen or the police;
We must love one another or die.

Defenceless under the night
90 Our world in stupor lies;
Yet dotted everywhere,
Ironic points of light
Flash out wherever the Just
Exchange their messages:
95 May I, composed like them
Of Eros and of dust,
Beleaguered by the same
Negation and despair,
Show an affirming flame.

99 ⸱ *The Shield of Achilles*

She looked over his shoulder
    For vines and olive trees,
Marble, well-governed cities
    And ships upon wine-dark seas;
5 But there on the shining metal
    His hands had put instead
An artificial wilderness
    And a sky like lead.

A plain without a feature, bare and brown,
10   No blade of grass, no sign of neighborhood,

Nothing to eat and nowhere to sit down;
  Yet, congregated on that blankness, stood
  An unintelligible multitude,
A million eyes, a million boots, in line,
Without expression, waiting for a sign.   15

Out of the air a voice without a face
  Proved by statistics that some cause was just
In tones as dry and level as the place;
  No one was cheered and nothing was discussed,
  Column by column, in a cloud of dust,   20
They marched away, enduring a belief
Whose logic brought them, somewhere else, to grief.

          She looked over his shoulder
            For ritual pieties,
          White flower-garlanded heifers,   25
            Libation and sacrifice:
          But there on the shining metal
            Where the altar should have been
          She saw by his flickering forge-light
            Quite another scene.   30

Barbed wire enclosed an arbitrary spot
  Where bored officials lounged (one cracked a joke)
And sentries sweated for the day was hot;
  A crowd of ordinary decent folk
  Watched from outside and neither moved nor spoke   35
As three pale figures were led forth and bound
To three posts driven upright in the ground.

The mass and majesty of this world, all
  That carries weight and always weighs the same,
Lay in the hands of others; they were small   40
  And could not hope for help, and no help came;
  What their foes liked to do was done; their shame
Was all the worst could wish: they lost their pride
And died as men before their bodies died.

171

45   She looked over his shoulder
            For athletes at their games,
        Men and women in a dance
            Moving their sweet limbs,
        Quick, quick, to music;
50   But there on the shining shield
        His hands had set no dancing-floor
        But a weed-choked field.

    A ragged urchin, aimless and alone,
        Loitered about that vacancy; a bird
55 Flew up to safety from his well-aimed stone:
        That girls are raped, that two boys knife a third,
    Were axioms to him, who'd never heard
    Of any world where promises were kept
    Or one could weep because another wept.

60   The thin-lipped armorer
            Hephaestos hobbled away;
        Thetis of the shining breasts
            Cried out in dismay
        At what the God had wrought
65   To please her son, the strong
        Iron-hearted man-slaying Achilles
            Who would not live long.

DYLAN THOMAS *1914-1953*

100 ♪ *A Winter's Tale*

        It is a winter's tale
    That the snow blind twilight ferries over the lakes
    And floating fields from the farm in the cup of the vales,
    Gliding windless through the hand folded flakes,
5   The pale breath of cattle at the stealthy sail,

        And the stars falling cold,
    And the smell of hay in the snow, and the far owl

172

Warning among the folds, and the frozen hold
Flocked with the sheep white smoke of the farm house cowl
In the river wended vales where the tale was told.   10

Once when the world turned old
On a star of faith pure as the drifting bread,
As the food and flames of the snow, a man unrolled
The scrolls of fire that burned in his heart and head,
Torn and alone in a farm house in a fold   15

Of fields. And burning then
In his firelit island ringed by the winged snow
And the dung hills white as wool and the hen
Roosts sleeping chill till the flame of the cock crow
Combs through the mantled yards and the morning men   20

Stumble out with their spades,
The cattle stirring, the mousing cat stepping shy,
The puffed birds hopping and hunting, the milk maids
Gentle in their clogs over the fallen sky,
And all the woken farm at its white trades,   25

He knelt, he wept, he prayed,
By the spit and the black pot in the log bright light
And the cup and the cut bread in the dancing shade,
In the muffled house, in the quick of night,
At the point of love, forsaken and afraid.   30

He knelt on the cold stones,
He wept from the crest of grief, he prayed to the veiled sky
May his hunger go howling on bare white bones
Past the statues of the stables and the sky roofed sties
And the duck pond glass and the blinding byres alone   35

Into the home of prayers
And fires where he should prowl down the cloud
Of his snow blind love and rush in the white lairs.
His naked need struck him howling and bowed
Though no sound flowed down the hand folded air   40

173

But only the wind strung
Hunger of birds in the fields of the bread of water, tossed
In high corn and the harvest melting on their tongues.
And his nameless need bound him burning and lost
45 When cold as snow he should run the wended vales among

The rivers mouthed in night,
And drown in the drifts of his need, and lie curled caught
In the always desiring centre of the white
Inhuman cradle and the bride bed forever sought
50 By the believer lost and the hurled outcast of light.

Deliver him, he cried,
By losing him all in love, and cast his need
Alone and naked in the engulfing bride,
Never to flourish in the fields of the white seed
55 Or flower under the time dying flesh astride.

Listen. The minstrels sing
In the departed villages. The nightingale,
Dust in the buried wood, flies on the grains of her wings
And spells on the winds of the dead his winter's tale.
60 The voice of the dust of water from the withered spring

Is telling. The wizened
Stream with bells and baying water bounds. The dew rings
On the gristed leaves and the long gone glistening
Parish of snow. The carved mouths in the rock are wind swept
   strings.
65 Time sings through the intricately dead snow drop. Listen.

It was a hand or sound
In the long ago land that glided the dark door wide
And there outside on the bread of the ground
A she bird rose and rayed like a burning bride.
70 A she bird dawned, and her breast with snow and scarlet downed.

Look. And the dancers move
On the departed, snow bushed green, wanton in moon light
As a dust of pigeons. Exulting, the grave hooved

Horses, centaur dead, turn and tread the drenched white
Paddocks in the farms of birds. The dead oak walks for love.   75

       The carved limbs in the rock
Leap, as to trumpets. Calligraphy of the old
Leaves is dancing. Lines of age on the stones weave in a flock.
And the harp shaped voice of the water's dust plucks in a fold
Of fields. For love, the long ago she bird rises. Look.   80

       And the wild wings were raised
Above her folded head, and the soft feathered voice
Was flying through the house as though the she bird praised
And all the elements of the slow fall rejoiced
That a man knelt alone in the cup of the vales,   85

       In the mantle and calm,
By the spit and the black pot in the log bright light.
And the sky of birds in the plumed voice charmed
Him up and he ran like a wind after the kindling flight
Past the blind barns and byres of the windless farm.   90

       In the poles of the year
When black birds died like priests in the cloaked hedge row
And over the cloth of counties the far hills rode near,
Under the one leaved trees ran a scarecrow of snow
And fast through the drifts of the thickets antlered like deer,   95

       Rags and prayers down the knee-
Deep hillocks and loud on the numbed lakes,
All night lost and long wading in the wake of the she-
Bird through the times and lands and tribes of the slow flakes.
Listen and look where she sails the goose plucked sea,   100

       The sky, the bird, the bride,
The cloud, the need, the planted stars, the joy beyond
The fields of seed and the time dying flesh astride,
The heavens, the heaven, the grave, the burning font,
In the far ago land the door of his death glided wide,   105

175

And the bird descended.
On a bread white hill over the cupped farm
And the lakes and floating fields and the river wended
Vales where he prayed to come to the last harm
110　　And the home of prayers and fires, the tale ended.

The dancing perishes
On the white, no longer growing green, and, minstrel dead,
The singing breaks in the snow shoed villages of wishes
That once cut the figures of birds on the deep bread
115　　And over the glazed lakes skated the shapes of fishes

Flying. The rite is shorn
Of nightingale and centaur dead horse. The springs wither
Back. Lines of age sleep on the stones till trumpeting dawn.
Exultation lies down. Time buries the spring weather
120　　That belled and bounded with the fossil and the dew reborn.

For the bird lay bedded
In a choir of wings, as though she slept or died,
And the wings glided wide and he was hymned and wedded,
And through the thighs of the engulfing bride,
125　　The woman breasted and the heaven headed

Bird, he was brought low,
Burning in the bride bed of love, in the whirl-
Pool at the wanting centre, in the folds
Of paradise, in the spun bud of the world.
130　　And she rose with him flowering in her melting snow.

A GLOSSARY OF
TECHNICAL TERMS

ALEXANDRINE: an iambic hexameter line; six iambic feet; twelve syllables. The commonest measure in classical French poetry and is often used in English verse for special effects along with iambic pentameters. An alexandrine concludes each of the stanzas of *The Faerie Queene*. (See SPENSERIAN STANZA.)

ALLEGORY: a narrative whose true meaning is discovered by translating its characters and actions into others which they are intended to symbolize. Bunyan's *Pilgrim's Progress* and Spenser's *The Faerie Queene* are the most famous allegories in English.

ALLITERATION: the repetition of consonants, or vowel sounds, particularly at the beginning of words and of stressed syllables. Examples:

> The breezes blew, the fair foam flew,
> The furrow followed free.
>> —Coleridge: *The Ancient Mariner*

> An Austrian army awfully arrayed
> Boldly by battery besieged Belgrade
>> —A. A. Watts: *The Siege of Belgrade*

> Pale beyond porch and portal
> Crowned with calm leaves she stands
>> —Swinburne: *The Garden of Proserpine*

ANAPEST: a metrical unit or foot, consisting of three syllables, two unstressed followed by one stressed. The following words are anapests: ascertain, introduce, anapest; and the following line from Byron's *The Destruction of Sennacherib* is made up of four anapests:

> And his co/horts were gleam/ing with pur/ple and gold.

ASSONANCE: the special effect resulting from the juxtaposition of identical or closely similar vowel sounds. Examples:

> Where palsy shakes a few sad last gray hairs
>> —Keats: *Ode to a Nightingale*

> The moan of doves in immemorial elms
>> —Tennyson: *The Princess*

It will be seen from this last example that assonance is often very effectively combined with alliteration in helping to make the sound of poetry expressive of the sense.

BALLAD: a poem meant for singing, which tells a story. The popular ballad, while probably originating with a single author, has been so added to and changed in the course of its passage from place to place and from one generation to another by word of mouth that it must be considered a communal production of the folk. The popular ballad presents a tragic view of life and is characterized by an absence of squeamishness, a sharp realism, and an acceptance of the consequences of evil, which give it a tragic dignity. Genuine folk ballads still appear in the modern world. Examples of these are *Casey Jones, Frankie and Johnny,* and *St. James Infirmary.*

BLANK VERSE: a series of unrhymed iambic pentameter lines. It is the verse form of the Elizabethan drama, of Milton's *Paradise Lost,* Wordsworth's *Tintern Abbey,* Tennyson's *Idylls of the King,* and many other modern narrative or reflective poems.

BURLESQUE: a satire in which a serious, grand, or elevated subject is treated with levity, as if it were mean or trivial. This is the reverse process from that found in the mock-heroic. (See MOCK-HEROIC.) Samuel Butler's *Hudibras* is a typical burlesque.

CACOPHONY: the jangling of harsh ugly sounds for the purpose of depicting something harsh and ugly or for expressing an attitude of repulsion, contempt, or disgust. Examples:

> Fans clap, silks rustle, and tough whalebones crack
> > —Pope: *The Rape of the Lock*

> With hatefullest disrelish writhed their jaws
> > —Milton: *Paradise Lost*

CAESURA: a 'cut' or break that divides a line of poetry into two parts. In some lines there is also a second minor break, as in the opening of Hamlet's famous soliloquy—

> To be,/or not to be;//that is the question.

Other illustrations are the following:

> And still she slept/an azure-lidded sleep
> > —Keats: *The Eve of St. Agnes*

> Farewell,/too little and too lately known
> > —Dryden: *To the Memory of Mr. Oldham*

CATALECTIC: a line of falling meter in which one or more of the final unstressed syllables are cut off is said to be *catalectic.* A complete line in which no syllables are cut off is said to be *acatalectic.*

> Take her up/tenderly   *acatalectic*
> Lift her with/care (˘)(˘)   *catalectic*
> > —Hood: *The Bridge of Sighs*

CLOSED COUPLET: a rhymed couplet in which the sense requires a marked pause at the end of each line. This is the common form of the heroic couplet in the eighteenth century, used with great effect in the satiric and didactic poems of Dryden and Pope. It may be contrasted with the open or run-on couplet as found in such poems as Browning's *My Last Duchess* or the satires and elegies of John Donne and Ben Jonson.

CONCEIT: an imaginative comparison making use of similes and metaphors in unexpected, surprising, or fantastic ways. The word is an older form of 'concept': a thought or idea. This was a form of wit much practiced in the seventeenth century and in some modern poetry in which an intellectual element is predominant. When successful this can be the source of powerful emotion. It has been defined by Dr. Johnson (in his *Life of Cowley*) as "a kind of *discordia concors*; a combination of dissimilar images, or discovery of occult resemblances in things apparently unlike."

CONSONANTAL RHYME: the matching of two pairs of consonants used in the place of the usual rhymes based on vowel sounds. Examples: grave, grieve; scope, skip; hot, hate. The English poet of the first world war, Wilfred Owen, used consonantal rhyme with great effect.

COUPLET, or DISTICH: a pair of lines linked by a rhyme. The commonest couplets are those of four feet (tetrameters), as in Marvell's *To his Coy Mistress,* and those of five feet (pentameters), as in Dryden's *To the Memory of Mr Oldham* or Browning's *My Last Duchess*. (See HEROIC COUPLET.)

DACTYL: a metrical unit or foot, consisting of three syllables, one stressed syllable followed by two unstressed syllables. The following words are dactyls: merrily, poverty, syllable; and the following lines from Thomas Hood's *The Bridge of Sighs* consist of two dactyls in each line (though in the second and fourth lines the two unstressed syllables of the final dactyl have been cut off. (See CATALECTIC.)

One more un/fortunate
 Weary of/breath (ᵛ) (ᵛ)
Rashly im/portunate
 Gone to her/death! (ᵛ) (ᵛ)

DIMETER: a line of two feet, such as the line *One more un/fortunate,* which consists of two dactyls.

DISTICH: See COUPLET.

DRAMATIC MONOLOGUE: a dynamic form of narrative in which the action and characterization are presented from the single point of view of one of the persons involved. Nothing is given but the words of this person. To whom he is speaking, under what circumstances, why and with what object the reader is left to discover as he goes through the poem. A dramatic monologue is distinguished from the soliloquy in that the speaker's words are addressed to someone other than himself. Robert Browning is the great master of this genre, *My Last Duchess* and *The Bishop Orders His Tomb* being brief and elegant examples of his skill.

ELEGY: originally a classic form of serious meditative verse, dealing with some aspect of death or love. In the sixteenth and seventeenth centuries the name was given to epistles, verse letters, and metaphysical love poems, such as those of Donne and Jonson. In modern times the name is restricted to a lyrical or reflective poem on death and mortality or a memorial poem on the death of a particular person. Milton's *Lycidas,* Gray's *Elegy Written in a Country Churchyard,* and Tennyson's *In Memoriam: A.H.H.* are the best known English elegies.

EPIC: a long narrative poem constructed on a grand scale, and celebrating in lofty verse the heroic deeds of men and gods. The ancient epic is of primitive origin, having taken form from cycles of ballads and lays preserved in an oral tradition. The classical epic is a reflection of racial and national ideals, a respository of myth and aspiration, the crystallization of the religious and patriotic ideals of a people. The finest examples of the primitive folk epic are the Greek poems assigned to Homer, the *Iliad* and the *Odyssey,* and in English literature, the Germanic epic *Beowulf.* Sophisticated literary imitations of the popular epic have, in the hands of a poet of genius, been made the richest and most serious of all types of poetry, with the possible exception of tragedy. Virgil's *Aeneid* and Dante's *Divine Comedy* represent the highest point reached by two great literatures; while Milton's *Paradise Lost* has a seriousness and magnificence shared only by the greatest of Shakespeare's tragedies.

EPIGRAM: a concise poem leading up to a witty or ingenious turn of thought. It has been defined and exemplified in a couplet by Coleridge:

What is an Epigram? A dwarfish whole;
Its body brevity, and wit its soul.

Some of the couplets in Pope's didactic poems can stand by themselves as perfect epigrams, as for example this memorable summing-up of neo-classic poetic theory:

True Wit is Nature to advantage dress'd;
What oft was thought, but ne'er so well express'd.

EPITAPH: a memorial verse intended to be carved on a tomb, or at least to commemorate the dead; and usually, whether dignified and serious or satirical and humorous, partaking of the brevity and wit of the epigram.

FALLING METER: a meter made up of feet in which the stressed syllables come first, e.g. trochees and dactyls. The unstressed syllable or syllables at the end of a line of falling meter may sometimes be omitted. (See CATALECTIC.)

FEMININE RHYME: See RHYME.

FIGURATIVE LANGUAGE: language that must be interpreted not literally but figuratively, i.e. imaginatively. The commonest figures of speech are the following, which see: HYPERBOLE, IRONY, METAPHOR, METONOMY, PERSONIFICATION, SIMILE, and SYNECDOCHE.

FOOT: the unit of rhythm. The commonest feet in English verse are the following: iamb (◡ —), trochee (— ◡), spondee (— —), anapest (◡◡—), and dactyl (—◡◡).

FREE VERSE, or vers libre: verse of an irregular metrical pattern. It is rhythmical, but the rhythm does not depend on the repetition of a regular series of feet but on a varying sequence of strophes. The Psalms and the Song of Solomon in the King James version of the Bible are free verse as are most of the poems of Walt Whitman.

HEROIC COUPLET: iambic pentameter lines rhymed in pairs. Heroic verse was that used in 'heroic' or epic poetry. In Greek and Latin poetry it was the hexameter; in French, the alexandrine; and in English, the iambic pentameter. The *Prologue* to *The Canterbury Tales* is one of the many poems by Chaucer in heroic couplets. The heroic couplet became very popular after the Restoration of 1660 and in the eighteenth century, when it was used in the 'heroic' plays of Dryden and others and in the satires and didactic poems of Dryden, Pope, and Johnson. The neo-classic couplet was generally end-stopped and consisted of a grammatically, logically, and rhetorically symmetrical statement well adapted for the epigrammatic expression of neatly discriminated ideas. For examples see Dryden's *To the Memory of Mr. Oldham* or Pope's *To a Young Lady on her Leaving the Town after the Coronation*.

HYPERBOLE: a figure of speech in which exaggeration is used for the sake of emphasis or irony. This is common in everyday speech, as when one says "You're killing me," as well as in poetry. Example:

Will all great Neptune's ocean wash this blood
Clean from my hand? Nay; this my hand will rather
The multitudinous seas incarnadine,
Making the green one red.

—Shakespeare: *Macbeth*

IAMB: a metrical foot consisting of two syllables, an unstressed one followed by a stress. The following words are iambs: afraid, accept, iamb. Because it is closest to the rhythm of ordinary speech, iambic lines are the most frequent in English poetry, iambic pentameters (lines of five iambic feet) forming blank verse when unrhymed and heroic couplets when arranged in rhyming pairs. The following line is an iambic pentameter:

The world/is too/much with/us; late/and soon.
—Wordsworth

IMAGERY: the collection of images within a poem; the references, whether literal or figurative, to objects discerned by the senses and which reciprocally communicate sensations, as of shape, size, color, or texture. Many images involve figures such as similes, metaphors, or personification, as in Wordsworth's

The holy time is quiet as a Nun
Breathless with adoration

or when Shakespeare refers to the sun as "the eye of Heaven" or says that "Summer's lease has all too short a date."

INTERNAL RHYME: a rhyming word or a series of rhyming words placed within the line, either with great regularity, as in this stanza from Shelley's *The Cloud*:

I bring fresh showers for the thirsting flowers,
From the seas and the streams;
I bear light shade for the leaves when laid
In their noonday dreams—

or more variously as in these lines from a song in Dryden's *Secular Masque*:

A very merry, dancing, drinking
Laughing, quaffing, and unthinking time.

IRONY: a figure that may be concentrated in a single epithet or extended as a kind of pervading spirit through the tone of a whole passage or a complete poem. This is the figure that implies the opposite of what is literally stated. Marvell's

The grave's a fine and private place,
But none, I think, do there embrace—

is a classic example of irony, as in a more extended form is Swift's essay *A Modest Proposal,* which proposes to cure the economic ills of overpopulated Ireland by butchering the babies of the poor and exporting them for the tables of the English upper classes.

LIGHT VERSE: verse, usually skilfully written and often in rigorous, complex, or elaborate forms, that avoids the deeper emotional and richer imaginative subjects and tones of 'serious' poetry and presents a cool, witty, intelligent, and frequently humorous expression of man as a social animal.

Light verse is frequently ironic, satirical, or critical and includes such forms and genres as the epigram, the limerick, nonsense poetry, and society verse. Such poets as Horace, Herrick, Pope, Lewis Carroll, Edward Lear, and Ogden Nash are masters of light verse.

LIMERICK: a facetious jingle, first popularised by Edward Lear. The strict form consists of five lines rhyming *aabba*. The *a* lines consist of eight syllables and the *b* lines of five. In earlier and less perfect examples the last line (or rhyme word) is a repetition of the first. Limericks have been composed on many subjects, including philosophical and theological ones. They are often satirical, ironic, nonsensical, ingenious, and indecent. A good one should have some unexpected and surprising 'turn' in the last line, as in the following:

> A gentleman dining at Kew
> Found a rather large mouse in his stew.
> > Said the waiter, "Don't shout
> > And wave it about,
> Or the rest will be wanting one too."

LYRIC: a general name given to all poetry that is predominantly musical or emotional. It excludes poems that are primarily narrative, didactic, satirical, or conversational; but such reflective poems as sonnets, elegies, and odes are usually included. The name is derived from the Greek lyre, which was used as an accompaniment to the reciting or chanting of the ode and elegy. The term is sometimes limited to the song—a short, unified, emotional poem intended to be sung to a musical accompaniment. Examples are the songs in Elizabethan dramas, Jonson's *Drink to me only with thine eyes,* Burns' *A Red, Red Rose,* or Verlaine's *Clair de Lune.*

MACHINERY: the supernatural beings (Olympian gods and goddesses or angels and demons) that play a part in epic poetry and in some mock-heroic poems.

MASCULINE RHYME: See RHYME.

METAPHOR: one of the most important figures of speech; it consists of a statement of identity, direct or implied, in which a thing, a person, an action, or a quality is affirmed to be some other unlike thing, person, action, or quality. Examples:

> Sweet spring, full of sweet days and roses,
> A box, where sweets compacted lie.
> > —Herbert: *Virtue*

> When the hounds of Spring are on winter's traces
> > —Swinburne: *Chorus from Atalanta in Calydon*

Robert Frost's sonnet *The Silken Tent* is one long brilliantly developed metaphor.

METAPHYSICAL POETRY: poetry, particularly that written in the seventeenth century by John Donne and his followers and in the twentieth century by T. S. Eliot, William Empson, Allen Tate, John Crowe Ransom and others, in which a strong and imaginative intellectual element finds expression in witty and fantastic conceits, whether as brief images or extended comparisons. Characteristic examples are found in Donne's comparison of absent lovers to the extended feet of a pair of compasses or in Eliot's image:

> —the evening is spread out against the sky
> Like a patient etherised upon a table.

Metaphysical poems included in this collection are Donne's *The Ecstasy,* Herbert's *The Pulley,* Marvell's *To his Coy Mistress,* and Hopkins' *The Windhover.* (See CONCEIT.)

METER: the regular repetition of an evenly spaced series of stressed syllables which distinguishes verse from prose. The metrical unit of English verse is the foot, consisting of either two or three syllables. (See FOOT, RHYTHM, and VERSE.)

METONOMY: a figure of speech in which an attribute or quality of a thing is named instead of the thing itself, as when *the Crown* is substituted for the monarch or *beauty* for beautiful women or beautiful things.

MOCK-HEROIC: a poem in which the ordinary or trivial is treated in a grand or elevated style as if it were of epic or heroic grandeur and seriousness. Pope's *The Rape of the Lock* is the most completely characteristic and successful example of the type. Little butterfly-like fairy creatures called Sylphs play the part in this mock epic that the gods and goddesses of Olympus play in the *Iliad* or the angels and devils in *Paradise Lost,* and a game of cards is described as though it were a battle.

MONOMETER: a line of one foot, as are the first, second, fourth, fifth, seventh, eighth, tenth, and eleventh lines of this stanza by Herrick:

> I must
> Not trust
> Here to any;
> Bereav'd,
> Deceiv'd
> By so many:
> As one
> Undone
> By my losses;
> Comply
> Will I
> With my crosses.

OCTAVE: the eight-line first stanza of the Italian sonnet. (See SONNET.)

OCTOSYLLABIC COUPLET: a rhyming couplet of four iambic feet; one of the most commonly found verse forms. Examples: Marvell's *To his Coy Mistress;* Milton's *L'Allegro* and *Il Penseroso;* and many of Chaucer's tales.

ODE: a reflective and more or less formal poem, usually of some length, exalted in tone and elaborate in style. Originally a choral interlude in Greek drama, it was divided into three parts, strophe, epode, and antistrophe in accordance with the conventional movements of a chorus of singers and dancers. Pindar developed the ode as an independent composition. Modern imitations of the Pindaric ode were written by Cowley, Dryden, Gray, Coleridge, Wordsworth, and others. The homostrophic ode (odes written in a single though often elaborate stanza) can be illustrated by Spenser's *Prothalamion,* Shelley's *Ode to the West Wind,* or the odes of Keats. Less elaborate, more familiar and more personal are the odes written in the manner of the Augustan poet Horace. Ben Jonson, Marvell, and Dryden wrote some fine odes in this manner. Pope's *Ode on Solitude* is a good example to be found in this book.

ONOMATOPOEIA: the special effect obtained by the use of words whose sound expresses their meaning. Such words are *crash, babble, bang, whirr, buzz.* More subtle examples are found in *lucent, syrup, lush, ooze,* etc. Onomatopoeic effects in verse depend on the use of such words and upon alliteration and assonance. (See ALLITERATION and ASSONANCE.) Some examples:

> Dry clash'd his harness in the icy caves
> And barren chasms, and all to left and right
> The bare black cliff clang'd round him . . .
> —Tennyson: *Morte d'Arthur*

> All side in parties, and begin th'attack:
> Fans clap, silks rustle, and tough whalebones crack.
> —Pope: *The Rape of the Lock*

> The coming musk-rose, full of dewy wine,
>   The murmurous haunt of flies on summer eves.
> —Keats: *Ode to a Nightingale*

> In Xanadu did Kubla Khan . . .
> —Coleridge: *Kubla Khan*

OTTAVA RIMA: a stanza invented by Boccaccio; the standard form of Italian heroic poetry; used by Byron in *Don Juan*. It is made up of eight iambic pentameter lines rhyming *abababcc*.

OXYMORON: the joining together in a single expression of ideas that are contradictory in a literal sense. The effect is one of surprise and emphasis. Example:

> Blind mouths!
> —Milton: *Lycidas*

PASTORAL POETRY: a classic and neo-classic genre in which an idealised and artificial picture of rural life and character is presented in an elegant and conventionalised style. The Greek poet Theocritus and the Roman poet Virgil are the classical masters of this kind of poetry. Spenser's *Shepherd's Calendar* and the *Pastorals* of Pope are the best examples of the genre in English. Some of the classic pastorals were funeral elegies in which the death of a real person was mourned in the guise of a dead shepherd. Milton's *Lycidas*, Keats' *Adonais,* and Arnold's *Thyrsis* are pastoral elegies of this sort.

PENTAMETER: a ten-syllable line; a line of five iambic, trochaic, or spondaic feet. The iambic pentameter is the commonest line in English verse, being the line found in blank verse and the heroic couplet.

PERSONIFICATION: a common figure of speech in which abstract qualities are spoken of as persons, either directly by being given a name and shown as acting or feeling as a person or indirectly by being given the attribute or power of a person or a god or other mythological being. Examples:

> Daughters of Time, the hypocrite Days
> > —Emerson: *Days*

> There Honour comes, a pilgrim gray
> > —Collins: *Ode, Written in the Year 1746*

> This sea that bares her bosom to the moon
> > —Wordsworth: Sonnet: *The World is Too Much With Us*

PINDARIC ODE: See ODE.

QUATRAIN: a stanza of four lines; the lines may be of any length and with any combination of one or two rhymes.

RHYME: the identity of sound between words or syllables extending from the end back to the last stressed vowel and no farther. The following words are perfect rhymes: *old* and *cold; older* and *colder; quality* and *jollity; Birmingham* and *confirming'em.* The beginning sound of rhyming syllables must be different: *station* and *crustacean, habit* and *inhabit* are not rhymes. 'Imperfect' rhymes such as *love* and *grove* or *hear* and *fare* are often used for special effect. One-syllable rhymes are called masculine; rhymes of more than one syllable are called feminine.

RHYTHM: a movement of discourse due to the alternation and variation of long and short or stressed and unstressed syllables. When this movement takes on a degree of regularity that can be seen as a recurring pattern of feet the discourse becomes verse and is said to be metrical. Prose and ordinary speech is not without rhythm, but the rhythm is too various to be described in terms of any regularly recurring pattern, i.e. it is not metrical. (See METER.)

RISING METER: a meter made up of feet in which the unstressed syllables come first, e.g., iambs and anapests.

RUN-ON LINES: lines in which there is no break in the sense or pause at the end of the line. The thought and the rhythm flow on from line to line; the break, or caesura, when it comes is within the line.

SESTET: the concluding six-line stanza of the Italian sonnet. (See SONNET.)

SIMILE: a figurative comparison in which two things actually unlike are stated to be like one another because a certain aspect or part can be thought of as having a significant similarity. Examples:

> Thy soul was like a Star; and dwelt apart.
> —Wordsworth: Sonnet: *Milton! Thou Shouldst Be Living At This Hour*
> My Luve is like a red, red rose.
> —Burns: *A Red, Red Rose*

A simile differs from a metaphor, to which it is akin, by stating a likeness or similarity, not an identity, usually by means of a comparative conjunction such as *like* or *as*. Note that the statement of an actual or literal likeness does not constitute a simile.

SONNET: a fourteen-line poem, reflective, personal, or dramatic, in which a rigorous conventional form is made to give added weight to the thought and feeling. There are two main types of sonnet: the Italian, or Petrarchan, and the English, or Shakespearean. The meter is usually iambic and the line a pentameter.

The Italian sonnet consists of two stanzas, the first of eight lines, called an octave, rhyming *abbaabba,* and the second of six lines called a sestet. Any combination of two or three rhymes is permitted here, *cdecde* and *cdcdcd* being two of the commonest. There should be a clear logical and emotional relationship between the octave and the sestet—a progression from the general to the particular, from the abstract to the concrete or *vice versa,* or from a particular experience to its interpretation or application. Wordsworth's *The World is Too Much With Us* is a fine example of the Italian sonnet, though not quite a perfect one: the break or 'turn' does not come at the end of the octave; the thought runs over to the end of the second foot of the ninth line. In such a sonnet as *On his Deceased Wife,* Milton disregards the break entirely and makes the sonnet a single developing entity with its climax in the fourteenth line.

The English sonnet is made up of three quatrains rhyming *abab, cdcd, efef,* and a concluding couplet, *gg.* The main division in the poem is at the end of the twelfth line. The final couplet is an epigrammatic summing-up of the point of the whole poem or a concentrated statement of its consequences. Shakespeare's three sonnets included in this collection or Keats' *Bright Star! Would I Were Steadfast As Thou Art* are English sonnets. Edmund Spenser varied the English sonnet by linking its three quatrains by means of an interlocking rhyme. The rhyme scheme of the Spenserian sonnet is *abab, bcbc, cdcd, ee.*

SPENSERIAN STANZA: a nine-line stanza, the first eight being iambic pentameters and the last an alexandrine (an iambic hexameter). The rhyme scheme is *ababbcbcc.* This stanza was first used by Edmund Spenser in *The Faerie Queene.* This stanza is found also in Thomson's *The Castle of Indolence,* Shelley's *Adonais,* Keats' *Eve of St. Agnes,* and can be seen here in the opening section of Tennyson's *The Lotos-Eaters.*

SPONDEE: a metrical foot of two syllables, both being stressed (book-case, key-ring, hair-do). This is used mainly as a substitution in an iambic line to slow up the speed or add weight and emphasis, as in Pope's illustrative line:

> When A/jax strives/some rock's/vast weight/to throw.

STRESS: beat or accent.

SUBSTITUTION: the varying of the normal metrical pattern of a line by the substitution of another kind of foot. The commonest substitutions are a trochee for an iamb at the beginning of a line or of a spondee for an iamb, variations illustrated in the first two lines of Keats' sonnet *Bright Star! Would I Were Steadfast As Thou Art:*

> Bright Star!/would I/were stead/fast as/thou art
> Not in/lone splen/dour hung/aloft/the night.

Substitution is one of the ways in which the mechanical sing-song effect of perfect regularity is avoided.

SYMBOL: in the most ordinary sense, a sign, picture, or object which stands for something else, the representation being figurative, not literal, e.g. the eagle may be a symbol of the United States, a cross of Christianity, or a rose of a beautiful woman. Symbols differ from ordinary images or metaphors in that they evoke more than an object or an idea: they evoke an attitude towards it and an emotion that accompanies it.

SYNECDOCHE: a figure of speech in which a part is named when the whole is to be understood, as in the phrase *all hands* meaning all the men of the crew or, conversely, as when we say *America* won the Davis Cup meaning the American team won.

TERCET: three lines linked by a single rhyme. Tennyson's *The Eagle* is made up of two tercets.

TERZA RIMA: a series of three-line stanzas connected by an interlocking rhyme, *aba, bcb, cdc,* etc. Dante's *Divine Comedy* and Shelley's *Ode to the West Wind* are terza rimas.

TETRAMETER: a line of four feet. Marvell's *To his Coy Mistress* consists of iambic tetrameter couplets.

TRIMETER: a line of three feet. The line *Ĭ ăm mŏn/arch ŏf all/Ĭ survey* is an anapestic trimeter.

TROCHEE: a metrical unit or foot consisting of two syllables, the first stressed and the second unstressed. Coleridge's line *Trochee/trips from/long to/ short* (˘) is a classic illustration.

VERSE: a word used in a number of different though related senses. (1) A line of poetry. (2) A stanza of a poem. (3) The short paragraph or strophe into which the chapters of the scriptures are divided. (4) Metrical writing as distinct from prose. (5) Metrical writing considered purely from a technical viewpoint. (6) Metrical writing which, intentionally or not, is less serious, emotional, exalted, imaginative, accomplished, or sincere than *poetry* is expected to be.

VERS LIBRE: See FREE VERSE.

Index of Authors and Titles

When a title is the same as the first line, it is indexed according to the first word, even if the first word is "The," "A," or "An."

A

B

C

G

H

I

J

K

L

W

Y